W9-BKC-174

Mario Batali

HOLIDAY FOOD

Mario Batali

HOLIDAY FOOD

Photographs by Quentin Bacon

CLARKSON POTTER/PUBLISHERS NEW YORK

TO SUSI, BENNO & LEO
THE SEA & THE SUN IN AMALFI

Published by Clarkson Potter/Publishers, New York, New York.
Member of the Crown Publishing Group.

Random House, Inc. New York, Toronto, London, Sydney, Auckland
www.randomhouse.com

Printed in the United States of America

Art Direction: Lisa Eaton
Design: Memo Productions/Lara Harris

Library of Congress Cataloging-in-Publication Data
Batali, Mario.
Mario Batali holiday food : family recipes for the most festive time of the year /
Mario Batali ; photographs by Quentin Bacon–1st ed.
Includes index.
I. Title: Holiday food. II. Title.
TX739.B36 2000
641.5′68–dc21 00-036308

ISBN 0-609-60774-X

10 9 8 7 6 5 4 3 2 1

First Edition

Acknowledgments

I would like to thank the following for their contributions to this book:

To my mom and dad and brother and sister for making every holiday something to celebrate;

To all of the chefs and cooks at Pó, Babbo, Lupa, and Esca, particularly Andy Nusser, Gina DePalma, Mark Ladner, John Baron, Jeff Butler, Patty Collins, John Eisenhart, Chris Juliano, Elisa Sarno, Jared Lewin, Dave Dibari, Memo Trevino, Jeff Burgess, Wade Moises, Adam Kopels, Kirsten Goldberg, Liz Chapman, Dan Latham, Sigrid Benedetti, and Jessica Lambert, who give me the time and opportunity to make books like this through their incredible work efforts and general excellence;

To all the floor staff in the front and back of the house at Pó, Babbo, Lupa, and Esca whose unflagging enthusiasm and knowledge creates joy at the table;

To my management team for thoughtful evaluation and leadership: Nancy Seltzer, Robert Amato, Rob Di Tursi, Erica Cantley, Scott Aseltine, and the two tall skinny ones;

To my partners Joe Bastianich, Jason Denton, Dave Pasternack, Lidia Bastianich, and Simon Dean for their attention to detail I cannot see.

To my editor Pam Krauss and her team, including Chloe Smith, Wendy Schuman, Marysarah Quinn, Amy Boorstein, and Teresa Nicholas for really making my scratchings a book;

To Lisa Eaton for style and grace on the page;

To Quentin Bacon and Tina Rupp for all of the visuals;

To Marina Malkin for her stylish table settings;

To Food Network for giving me a podium;

To Jim Harrison for inspiration, syncopation, and appetite;

To Rita, Maurizio, and Bruno deRosa for explaining *la vera cucina Napoletana* with passion and joy;

To my assistant Laurie Woolever for keeping my world in order;

To Tony Gardner and Cathy Frankel for fighting the lions;

To Sergio Esposito and the team at Italian Wine Merchants for creating a festive place for interaction;

To the restaurant community in New York City, all of the chefs, cooks, proprietors, managers, waiters, sommeliers, bus people, and dish washers who make it a constant joy to live and work and breathe in this exquisitely rich environment;

And to all of the customers at Pó, Babbo, Lupa, Esca, and Italian Wine Merchants whose support allows me to dream.

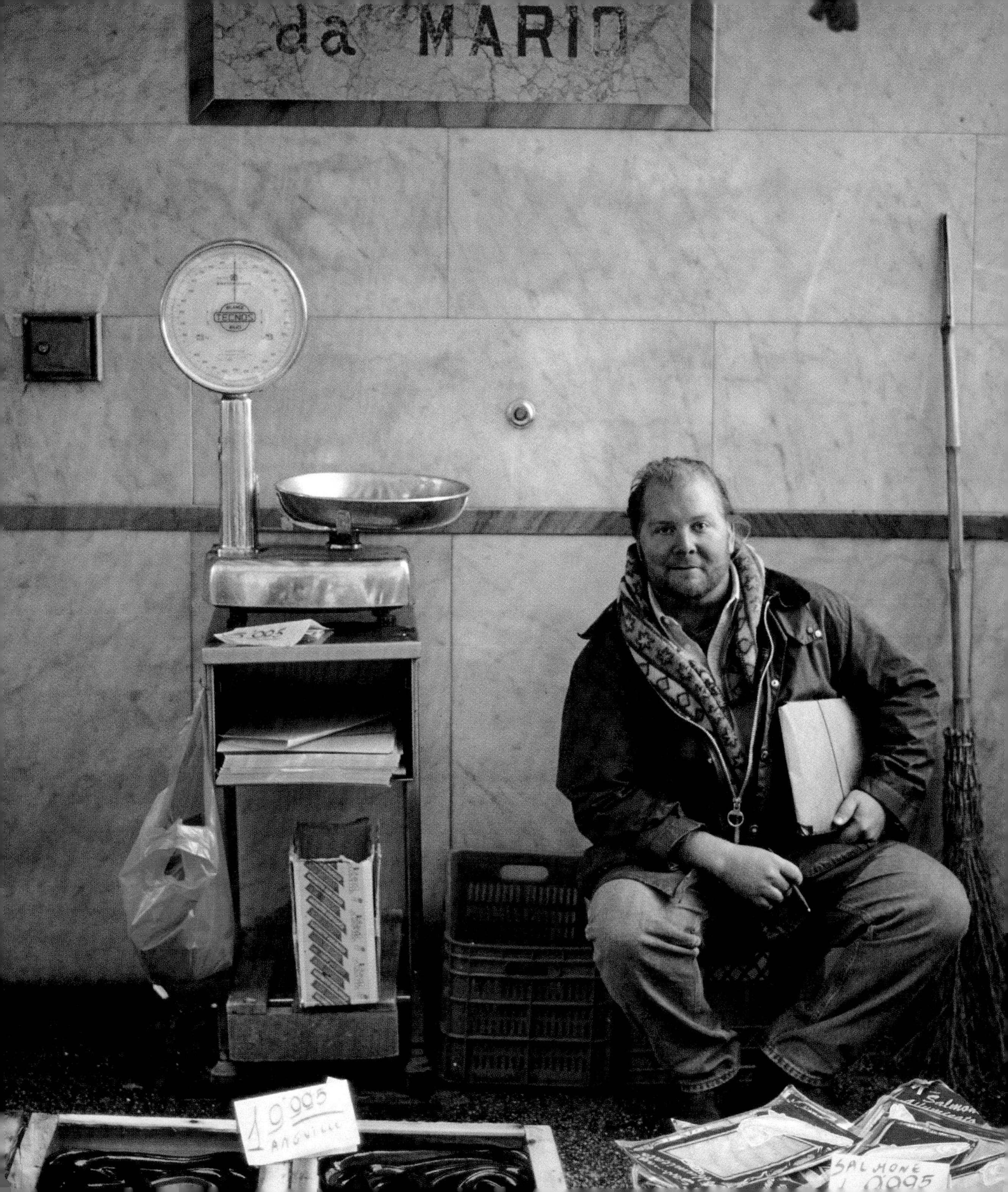
da MARIO
ANGUILLE
SALMONE

CONTENTS

ALIMENTARI
CARRANO

HOLIDAY FOOD

Some of the world's most delicious traditions come out of Italian homes, and never is this more apparent than at the holidays, when every grandma, aunt, cousin, and mother contributes her renowned specialties to the family table. Holidays in Italy are numerous, and quite frequently observed with special regional delicacies. At Christmastime and Easter, however, the food fest becomes a national obsession. Some days huge spreads of incredibly beautiful and delicious comestibles are on tap; on other days it may be just two or three deeply significant dishes, the recipes passed down through generations. This is not to say that everyone celebrates the same way or with the same dishes; each region (indeed, each household) has its own specialties and rituals, all of them irresistibly good. ✳ Perhaps the best known of these annual holiday meals is La Vigilia, also known as the Feast of Seven Fishes. This legendary repast is replete with seafood served in every style imaginable, from baked and fried to chilled in a salad or stuffed into pasta. The actual selection of dishes, and the number served, varies from house to house, but any one of them would be a showstopper for a casual meal with friends; presented together, they provide a memorable feast. Other days might feature a conventional meat entrée at the center, supplemented by a tempting roster of antipasti, pastas, and contorni. And throughout this festive time there are cookies and other irresistible sweet treats. ✳ Growing up in the Pacific Northwest, I saw my Italian-American family meld traditions from both cultures. We began planning the holidays by the end of October: Thanksgiving at our house, Christmas Eve at Grandma Batali's, New Year's Eve at home again,

Christmas time…
the most magical and
special holiday
of the whole year.

the big bowl games with Uncle Dick and Aunt Marty, Super Bowl Sunday in the neighborhood. Any meals served at our house were mapped out at least a month in advance, down to any rentals we'd need and the beverages to be served, from California or local Washington wine to eggnog or Tom and Jerrys (both plain or fortified). We'd plan every possible opportunity to relax and enjoy a bite of salami, or sip fresh cider, or snatch a cookie from the huge box Grandma sent each year. We'd shop and cook as a family, with the belief that most things homemade are superior to store-bought. We flavored grappa, cured our own olives, made all the cookies and decorations for our Christmas tree. We did all this, not out of need, but out of pride and respect for custom, and also because the joy of creating good things together is what great traditions and holidays are all about. ✳ For many of these meals we relied on recipes that have always been part of my family's traditions, both because we enjoyed the continuity they represented and because the truly joyous spirit of Italian generosity and festivity seemed right for the holidays. ✳ Many of these dishes remain on the holiday menu in my own home today. I wouldn't consider it Christmas Eve without a dish of glazed eels and a plate of tiny struffoli to nibble afterward. Likewise, no New Year's spread would be complete without a platter of lentils and sausage, a traditional talisman for prosperity in the year to come. But over the years, as I've had the good fortune to live in and travel through Italy, discovering the fascinating diversity of its regional cuisines, I've continued to expand the roster of holiday dishes. ✳ At this time of the year in particular I look to the food of Campania, more specifically the Amalfi coast between Naples and Salerno, where simply prepared seafood and produce epitomize what I love and admire about Italian cooking–just as the picaresque Neapolitan character and the intensity of life spirit there echo what I like best about the Italian people. The stunning scenery makes the Amalfi coast one of Italy's most memorable tourist destinations, but it is the food that draws me back, time after time. Many of the dishes I've enjoyed at tiny, family-run trattorias or at the tables of locals who have generously invited me into their homes, are now annual occurrences at my holiday gatherings. ✳ The recipes that follow are representative of what you might encounter in an Italian home during this festive time, some of them my own variations

"Many of the gifts at my house were gastronomic."

and others purely traditional. Don't feel obligated to follow the lineup exactly. An Italian household would certainly offer three pastas on an important holiday, but if your crowd wants only one, by all means trim the menu. ✳ With the possible exception of the labor-intensive Christmas Eve dinner, these meals would be ideal for any holiday celebration. The Christmas Day menu could easily translate into a Thanksgiving feast of spectacular proportions. The New Year's Day meal would be a perfect Super Bowl Sunday spread. Even in Italian homes, the specifics of ingredients may vary from year to year. Someone's Grandma might suggest that no true recipe for Christmas cookies uses honey. Or that the New Year's Eve menu shouldn't have cotecchino sausage but must include raisins. Or that no one makes the baccalà with mint. These are the little disputes and quibbles that make eating in Italian or Italian-American homes so much fun. The best thing is that everyone is right: family traditions are all correct–it's the food that makes it work. ✳ With each menu I've also included a *regali*, or gift, quick takes on favorite holiday eats and treats, and an aperitivo–that is to say, something to get the juices going before the actual meal. We tend to snack all day on little antipastilike salami and cheese or pickled vegetables, and having a small sip to go with them is very Italian. Whether this happens in the kitchen when you start preparing the meal in the morning or early afternoon or when the guests arrive before dinner is entirely up to you. ✳ Of course the Italian holidays are not just a series of huge, elaborate meals. These times are spent with the children in the room, and with the oldest of aunts playing a central role in family affairs. The Batali tradition of spending Christmas Eve in a house lit entirely by candlelight is one of my most vivid memories of childhood and one that I treasure. ✳ So make it easy on yourself. Choose dishes that you can prepare at least partially in advance or that your family can help with. Make the Christmas tree decorations in October, make the grappa in November, make the cookies the week before. The most important part of holiday get-togethers is exactly that: getting together. So either plan it so you can get out of the kitchen, or get everyone else in there with you. *Buone Feste!* ✳

Me with my parents, brother, and sister.
Opposite: *Trimming the tree.*

A NOTE ABOUT THE YIELDS IN THIS BOOK

You'll note that many of these recipes indicate a range of servings. In such instances, the smaller yield represents *an American-style entrée portion.* If they are to be served as part of a large buffet spread or a multicourse Italian meal, they will serve more. A pasta dish, for example, that yields 4 to 8 servings may even serve 10 if offered along with one or more additional pastas and multiple courses but only 4 if served as the main event. A good rule of thumb is 4 ounces of pasta per adult for an American-style serving, 2 to 3 ounces for a multicourse Italian portion. The antipasti represent appetizer-size portions, but these, too, will serve at least as many as the larger number indicated if offered as part of a large spread. The same is true of most of the desserts. The aperitivo recipes can be multiplied up or down as needed.

THE WINES OF CAMPANIA

Many of the recipes in this book were inspired by a recent trip Mario and I took to the Amalfi coast, a beautiful stretch of seaside in the heart of Campania. In Campania, everyone cooks nonstop from Christmas on through New Year's, scuttling around the city looking for the most pungent baccalà, the freshest eels, and the sea bass with the clearest-looking eyes. Yet somehow, amid the swirl of activity, people always manage to find time for a quick *quartino di vino.* Typically, that wine will come with a side of fizzy water, to spritz it up a bit and dilute its alcohol bite. ✳ Campania's wines, white and red, are not about big juicy fruit and loads of oak; they are firm and fine, with a mouthwatering acidity that makes them ideal partners for food. The region's pristine seafood is perfectly matched by lean, palate-cleansing whites like Lacryma Christi (which means "Tears of Christ") and Fiano di Avellino. The regional pasta specialties call out for tart, fragrant reds made from Aglianico, the signature red grape of Campania, as well as other local varieties such as Piedirosso and Primitivo. ✳ Campania's long coast is dotted with wine zones where the fertile volcanic soils are better known for tomatoes, peaches, and lemons than for grapes. Generally speaking, serious wine drinkers have to look inland for *vini* of more depth and complexity than the light coastal wines. That search leads inevitably to the foggy, precipitous hills near the town of Avellino, where the three contiguous wine zones of Fiano di Avellino, Greco di Tufo, and Taurasi turn out Campania's most heralded wines. ✳ Regardless of the menu you're serving–be it the more luxurious feasts of the manor homes in the Vomero *quartiere* or a down-home fish fry–there are Campanian wines to suit your needs. Start your guests off with some seafood salad and a crisp Fiano or Greco, then move on to something heartier to pair with an Aglianico-based red. The wine recommendations I've included for Mario's recipes place an emphasis on the indigenous grape varieties, and some of them are small-production wines that can be hard to find. But for the authentic Campanian experience, these are the wines to seek out. ✳

by Joseph V. Bastianich

CAMPANIA'S DOC ZONES

Italian wine law classifies wines in several different ways. The categories are: Vino da Tavola, or VDT (usually simple table wine, but sometimes more high-end wine that is made from nonapproved grape varieties, e.g., the "Super Tuscans"); Indicazione Geographica Tipica, or IGT (established in 1992 to distinguish wines made in a specific geographic area, but perhaps from grapes or methods not approved by the government for that region); Denominazione di Origine Controllata, or DOC (denomination of controlled origin–the wine must come from a specific growing area, and adhere to certain production methods and aging requirements; there are more than 300 DOCs in Italy); and DOCG (denomination of controlled and guaranteed origin, a step up from DOC; there are now 21 throughout Italy).

Campania has a total of nineteen DOC zones. Key grapes in the wines are listed in parentheses:

Aglianico del Taburno/Taburno (reds: Aglianico; whites: Coda di Volpe, Falanghina, Greco)

Asprinio di Aversa (whites: Asprinio)

Campi Flegrei (reds: Piedirosso; whites: Falanghina)

Capri (reds: Piedirosso; whites: Falanghina, Greco)

Castel San Lorenzo (reds: Barbera, Sangiovese; whites: Malvasia Bianca, Trebbiano Toscano)

Cilento (reds: Aglianico, Piedirosso, Primitive; whites: Fiano, Greco, Trebbiano)

Costa d'Amalfi (reds: Piedirosso; whites: Falanghina)

Falerno del Massico (reds: Aglianico, Piedirosso, Primitivo; whites: Falanghina)

Fiano di Avellino (whites: Fiano)

Greco di Tufo (whites: Greco)

Guardiolo (reds: Aglianico, Sangiovese; whites: Falanghina)

Ischia (reds: Piedirosso; whites: Biancolella)

Peninsola Sorrentina (reds: Aglianico, Piedirosso; whites: Biancolella, Falanghina, Greco)

Sant'Agata De'Goti (reds: Aglianico, Piedirosso; whites: Falanghina, Greco)

Solopaca (reds: Aglianico, Sangiovese; whites: Coda di Volpe, Falanghina)

Taurasi (Campania's only DOCG; red: Aglianico)

Vesuvio (reds: Piedirosso; whites: Coda di Volpe, Falanghina, Greco, Verdeca)

CHRISTMAS

EVE

Christmas Eve was probably the most exciting night of the year for us children. We put the finishing touches on our gifts to each other and our parents, and plotted the beverage and cookie options for Santa. (This would later morph into a disgusting beverage of the most toxic proportions we could challenge him with.) We finished the last-minute details of our notes to Santa, made sure we'd chosen the largest stocking in the drawer, and counted the gifts already under the tree with our names on them. Our Christmas Eve dinner was usually eaten at Grandma Batali's table, and involved an assortment of dishes we had not seen all year—at least since last Christmas Eve, some of which I found challenging as a child. I have, later in life, grown to love many of the suspicious things on the Italian table, and many of those "challenging" dishes are now present at my table, as well as other dishes I have picked up in my travels. The tradition of the seven, or ten, or thirteen fishes at Christmas Eve, or La Vigilia, was one of the mysteries I set out to uncover when I started writing this book, and I must admit that, owing to one of the

APERITIVO

BLOOD ORANGE BELLINI

ANTIPASTI

ALICI MARINATI
Marinated Fresh Anchovies

BROCCOLI SOFFRITI
Braised Broccoli

VONGOLE ORIGANATE
Clams with Oregano and Bread Crumbs

CAPITONE MARINATO
Marinated Eel

PASTA

LINGUINE CON LE VONGOLE
Linguine with Clams

RAVIOLI ALLA SPIGOLA
Sea Bass Ravioli with Marjoram and Potatoes

SPAGHETTI ALLE COZZE
Spicy Spaghetti with Mussels

SECONDI

BACCALÀ ALLA VESUVIANA
Salt Cod with Capers, Mint, and Chiles

GAMBERONI AL' ACQUA PAZZA
Shrimp in "Crazy Water"

ARAGOSTE ALLE BRACE
Grilled Lobster with Lemon Oil and Arugula

DOLCI

CROCCANTE
Almond Brittle

CANNOLI DI RICOTTA
Classic Cannoli

STRUFFOLI
Tiny Honey-Covered Fritters

ZEPPOLE
Italian Doughnuts

REGALI: GIFTS OF FOOD
Grappa Cherries, Marinated Mushrooms, Panettone, Flavored Olives

most beautiful and yet difficult aspects of Italian food culture and lore, I cannot report a complete success. This is because the Italian family tradition is so strong and yet so individually based that there are few things, up to and including the preparation of after-dinner coffee, that everyone can possibly agree on. I've heard that seven is the number because there are seven sacraments in the Catholic Church. Or that the number is ten for the ten Stations of the Cross. Or that it is thirteen for the number of apostles plus Jesus. Regardless of the number, deck the house with your best things because it's Christmas Eve, the family is all here, and it's all about love.

WINE RECOMMENDATIONS

For a fun, easy-drinking white to sip while unpacking groceries, cooking, and general household bantering, pour a Lacryma Christi Bianco, Mastroberardino, a 100% Coda Di Volpe. Vadiaperti's Fiano di Avellino is a well-structured honey-nut white that's perfect for first course seafood and bready appetizers; Vadiaperti is known for the elegance and consistency of their Fiano from one vintage to the next. Albente, Feudi Di San Gregori offers a perfect blend of structure, style, and fruit, with enough weight to come alive with seafood-based primi. The 50/50 blend of Greco Di Tufo and Coda Di Volpe gives it both backbone and approachability to ride the line between serious and fun. For the main event, choose Greco Di Tufo, Santa Agata dei Goti, Mustilli. Spending some time in French oak gives this wine a weighty structure that puts Campania's indigenous varietal on a par with the best white wines of the world.

BLOOD ORANGE BELLINI

Place champagne flutes in the freezer for 20 minutes. Open the prosecco and let it stand in an ice bucket for 5 minutes.

Pour ¼ cup of blood orange juice into each glass. Fill to within ½ inch of the top of the glass with prosecco (about 4 ounces) and serve.

1 bottle **prosecco** (sparkling Italian wine), chilled

2 cups **blood orange juice** frozen or freshly squeezed from about 15 blood oranges

Serves 8

ALICI MARINATI

Marinated Fresh Anchovies

2 pounds fresh **anchovies**

2 cups **white wine vinegar**

2 cups extra-virgin **olive oil**

2 tablespoons dried **oregano**

2 tablespoons hot red **pepper flakes**

¼ cup finely chopped **Italian parsley**

4 **garlic cloves,** sliced paper-thin

2 tablespoons **sea salt**

Lemon wedges (optional)

Makes approximately 48 fillets; serves 8

One bite of this exemplary antipasto entirely changed the way I thought about Italian cooking—and cooking in general. So Zen-like in their elegance and simplicity, so little and yet so much said, these delicious little dreamboats truly capture the dreamlike state of the Amalfi coast and the cooking that defines it.

The cured anchovies will keep in the refrigerator for up to one week.

Using scissors, trim the fins off of all the anchovies. Using a sharp paring knife, slit each fish along the belly from head to tail; remove the entrails and rinse well. Cut off the heads and carefully pull out the spine and pin bones from the top with your index finger and thumbnail. Separate the two fillets and rinse again. Arrange a layer of the fillets in a deep oval gratin dish and sprinkle with a tablespoon or two of vinegar.

Continue until all the fish fillets are used, then pour the rest of the vinegar over the fish. Cover and marinate in the fridge for at least 4 hours.

Remove the anchovies from the vinegar, rinse, and pat dry with a kitchen towel. Wash out the dish and dry well. Return a single layer of cured anchovies to the dish and sprinkle with 2 or 3 tablespoons olive oil, a pinch of oregano, a pinch of pepper flakes, a pinch of parsley, three or four garlic slices, and a pinch of salt. Layer in the rest of the anchovies, sprinkling each layer with oil, oregano, pepper flakes, parsley, garlic, and salt. Cover again and marinate in the fridge for at least 2 hours.

To serve, bring anchovies to just below room temperature (in Italy they would be served at about 58°F). Remove from the oil and arrange six or seven on each plate with a lemon wedge if desired.

BROCCOLI SOFFRITI

Braised Broccoli

This dish is to Christmas Eve dinner in Amalfi what apple pie is to July Fourth in middle America: an absolute necessity. The Amalfitani choose a leafy, lighter colored broccoli from Campania for this dish; the closest substitute in this country is broccoli rabe; choose a bunch with as many leaves as possible.

3 pounds fresh **broccoli rabe,** with leaves, if possible, or 3 pounds **broccoli**

¼ cup extra-virgin **olive oil**

8 **garlic cloves,** halved

10 marinated **anchovy fillets,** roughly chopped (page 22) or 5 salted-packed anchovies, soaked, rinsed and filleted (see Note)

Kosher salt and freshly ground **black pepper**

¼ cup **toasted bread crumbs**

Serves 8

Trim the broccoli rabe into long stalks, removing the bottom 2 inches and leaving the leaves attached. Bring 6 quarts of water to a boil. Meanwhile, place a 12- to 14-inch sauté pan over medium-low heat and add the olive oil. Add the garlic and anchovies and cook 5 minutes, stirring often, until just golden brown and very fragrant. While the garlic and anchovies cook, plunge the broccoli rabe into the boiling water and cook for 1 minute. Drain the broccoli rabe well and add it to the pan with the garlic and anchovies. Cook over low heat for 10 to 12 minutes, until tender but still holding its shape. Remove from heat and season aggressively with pepper and timidly with salt. Serve hot or at room temperature sprinkled with the bread crumbs.

Anchovies

Whenever anchovies are called for in my recipes, the quantity is given as a number of fillets—preferably taken from fresh anchovies you have marinated yourself (see page 22), which yield two fillets each. If prepackaged anchovies must be used, however, be aware that they come in one acceptable—and one despicable—form. Salt-packed anchovies that come in a 1- or 2-kilo can are available in Italian delis and are sold whole. Order them by the quarter-pound, take them home, soak them in either water or milk, then remove the fillets. Least desirable are the tiny cans of salty prefilleted anchovies packed in oil. This is not to say that all brands of canned fillets are not very good, but most aren't, so use one of the other types if you can.

VONGOLE ORIGANATE

Clams with Oregano and Bread Crumbs

24 medium **littleneck clams,** scrubbed

3 cups **kosher salt**

4 tablespoons extra-virgin **olive oil,** plus extra for drizzling

1 medium **red onion,** cut into $^1/_8$-inch dice

4 **garlic cloves,** thinly sliced

1 **red bell pepper,** cut into $^1/_8$-inch dice

1 cup fresh **bread crumbs**

Kosher salt and freshly ground **black pepper**

2 tablespoons chopped fresh **oregano**

Serves 4 to 8

This "red sauce meets Guido in Little Italy" classic has much more to do with the clams than what you may be used to eating. Note that the bread crumbs here are fresh—that is to say, made only from today's bread, not from day-old bread (and definitely not the kind that comes in a can).

Carefully open the clams, discarding the top shells, and drain the clam liquid into a small mixing bowl. Set aside. Loosen the clams from the bottom shells but do not remove them. Pour the salt onto a baking sheet so that it is at least a ½-inch deep and arrange the clams in their half-shells in the salt.

In a 10- to 12-inch sauté pan, heat the oil over medium heat until smoking. Add the onion, garlic, and bell pepper and cook 6 to 7 minutes, until softened and light golden brown. Add the bread crumbs and continue cooking another 3 minutes, until they are light golden brown as well. Remove the mixture from the heat, season with salt and pepper, and cool. Stir in the oregano and the reserved clam liquid.

Preheat the broiler. Pack about 2 teaspoons of the crumb mixture loosely into each clam shell. (Remember that the clam, not the stuffing, is the most important part of this dish; stuffing should surround and enhance the clam, not overpower it.)

Place the clams under the broiler and heat through, about 1½ to 2 minutes, just until the crumb mixture is deep golden brown; you're not really cooking the clam. Drizzle with a drop of olive oil, and serve.

CAPITONE MARINATO

Marinated Eel

This dish is a prerequisite for any serious attempt at a traditional Italian Christmas Eve table. Even my most squeamish friends admit to liking this dish once I've tricked them into tasting it. If you have a hard time finding eel at your fancy fishmonger, try the local Chinatown, where eel is considered a delicacy all year long. (Although you can substitute Chilean sea bass if you insist.)

3 cups **red wine vinegar**

6 **garlic cloves,** peeled and slightly crushed but left whole

1 cup **sugar**

6 cups extra-virgin **olive oil,** for frying

1 3-pound **eel,** peeled by your fishmonger, or 3 pounds rich, firm fish fillet like Chilean sea bass, black cod, or grouper

Kosher salt and freshly ground **black pepper**

1 cup all-purpose **flour**

3 tablespoons chopped fresh **oregano**

¼ cup best-quality extra-virgin **olive oil,** for drizzling

3 tablespoons fresh **marjoram leaves**

Serves 8

In a nonreactive saucepan, combine the vinegar, garlic, and sugar and bring to a boil. Cook until reduced by one-third to 2 cups, about 20 minutes. Remove from heat and allow to cool.

Heat the 6 cups of oil to 375°F in a large, deep pot. If the oil is not 4 to 5 inches deep, add enough oil to bring it to that level.

Cut the eel into 2-inch by 1-inch pieces, season with salt and pepper, and dredge in the flour.

Carefully drop three or four pieces of fish at a time into the oil and cook 5 to 6 minutes, until light golden brown and cooked through. With a slotted spoon, transfer to paper towels to drain, then place gently into a large salad bowl.

Pour the vinegar reduction over the fish, sprinkle with oregano, cover with plastic wrap, and refrigerate for at least 4 hours or up to 2 days.

Remove from the refrigerator 1 hour before serving. Drizzle with olive oil, sprinkle with marjoram leaves, and serve.

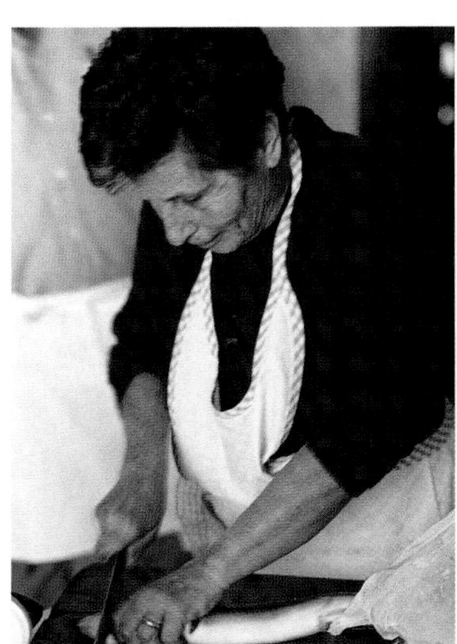

LINGUINE CON LE VONGOLE

Linguine with Clams

3 tablespoons extra-virgin **olive oil**

4 **garlic cloves,** thinly sliced

1 pound New Zealand **cockles,** or 24 **Manila clams,** scrubbed and rinsed

½ cup dry **white wine**

1 cup canned **plum tomatoes,** roughly chopped with their juices

1 tablespoon hot red **pepper flakes**

1 pound **linguine**

½ cup finely chopped **Italian parsley**

Serves 4 to 8

This is red clam sauce at its cleanest and most honest. Any type of fresh small shellfish could be substituted for the clams, and substitutions abound in Amalfi, where the fishermen truly decide what appears on the daily table. Generally all shellfish are served in their shells.

To Italians, the carpet-shell clams, or *Venerupis decussata,* are the "true clams," or *vongole verace.* Other similar species, commonly substituted, include *vongole gialle* (golden carpet-shell clams) and *tartufi di mare* (truffles of the sea). Cockles or Manila clams make fine stand-ins.

Bring 8 quarts of water to a boil in a large pasta pot and add 3 tablespoons of salt.

In a 14- to 16-inch skillet, heat the oil and garlic over medium heat until the garlic is golden brown. Add the clams, wine, tomatoes, and pepper flakes, cover, and cook 7 to 8 minutes, until all the clams have just opened.

Meanwhile, drop the pasta into the salted water and cook according to the package directions to 1 minute short of al dente. It should still be quite firm. Reserve 1 cup of the pasta water, then drain the pasta in a colander and pour immediately into the skillet with the clams.

Cook over high heat for 45 seconds. Stir in the parsley, add some of the reserved pasta water if the pasta seems too dry, and serve in a large bowl.

RAVIOLI ALLA SPIGOLA

Sea Bass Ravioli with Marjoram and Potatoes

PASTA DOUGH

3½ to 4 cups all-purpose **flour,** plus ½ cup for dusting

4 extra-large **eggs**

1 tablespoon extra-virgin **olive oil**

FILLING

13 tablespoons extra-virgin **olive oil**

2 **garlic cloves,** thinly sliced

1 pound boneless, skinless **sea bass fillet** (or any flavorful firm fish such as sole, halibut, grouper), flesh cut in ½-inch cubes

5 tablespoons chopped fresh **marjoram leaves**

1 large baking **potato,** boiled, peeled, and mashed

Kosher salt and freshly ground **black pepper**

1 cup **Basic Tomato Sauce** (page 97)

Serves 4 to 8

To prepare these as they are made in Amalfi—or anywhere in Campania—you need a rolling pin with the ravioli shape stamped into the rolling surface. As these are sometimes difficult to find, I have provided alternative instructions.

Mound the flour in the center of a large board. Make a well in the middle and add the eggs and oil. Using a fork, beat eggs and oil, then begin to incorporate the flour, starting with the inner rim of the well. The dough will come together when half of the flour is incorporated. Keep working the dough until all the flour is incorporated.

Start kneading the dough with both hands, using the palms of your hands. Once you have a cohesive mass, remove the dough from the board and scrape up and discard any leftover bits. Lightly reflour the board and continue kneading for 6 more minutes. The dough should be elastic and a little sticky. Wrap the dough in plastic and allow to rest for 30 minutes at room temperature. Do not skip the kneading or resting portion of this recipe.

In a 12- to 14-inch sauté pan, heat 4 tablespoons of the oil until it is smoking. Add the garlic and cook until light golden brown, about a minute. Add the fish pieces and sauté, stirring constantly, until fish is just cooked through, about 8 or 9 minutes. Remove to a mixing bowl and allow to cool. Add 3 tablespoons of chopped marjoram, the potato, and 6 tablespoons of oil and stir to mix well, being certain to break up the fish pieces. Season to taste with salt and pepper and set aside.

Roll out pasta to the thinnest setting and place on a lightly floured surface. If you have a ravioli cutting rolling pin, cover the pasta with a ¼-inch-thick layer of the sea bass mixture. Place a second sheet of pasta over it and press down lightly with your hands. Carefully roll the two sheets together with the roller to form the ravioli. Use a pastry cutter to cut the ravioli apart.

Alternatively, cut a single sheet of pasta at a time into rectangles 2 inches by 1 inch. Place a teaspoon of the fish mixture into the center of each rectangle and fold the pasta to form a 1-inch square, pressing the edges to seal. Repeat until dough or stuffing is finished.

Bring 8 quarts of water to a boil and add 3 tablespoons salt. Drop the ravioli in and cook until tender, 6 to 7 minutes. Meanwhile place tomato sauce in a 12- to 14-inch sauté pan. Add the 3 tablespoons of remaining oil and 2 tablespoons of marjoram leaves and place over medium heat. Drain the ravioli, reserving a cup of the cooking water, add to the pan with the tomato sauce, and toss to dress. Adjust the consistency of the sauce with pasta water and serve immediately.

SPAGHETTI ALLE COZZE

Spicy Spaghetti with Mussels

Mussels are an inexpensive shellfish that are too often overlooked in the seafood case. When properly cooked, as in this dish, they are delicious and make a dramatic (and very Christmas-y) presentation, with flecks of green and red.

6 tablespoons extra-virgin **olive oil**

3 **garlic cloves,** thinly sliced

2 **red bell peppers,** cored, seeded, and cut into ¼-inch dice

1 tablespoon hot red **pepper flakes**

24 Prince Edward Island **mussels,** scrubbed and rinsed

1½ cups **dry white wine**

1 pound **spaghetti**

¼ cup finely chopped **Italian parsley**

Serves 4 to 8

Bring 6 quarts of water to a boil and add 2 tablespoons salt.

In a 12- to 14-inch sauté pan, heat the oil over medium-high heat until just smoking. Add the garlic, bell peppers, and pepper flakes and cook until soft, 7 to 8 minutes. Add the mussels and cook 1 minute, stirring regularly. Add the wine and bring to a boil. Meanwhile drop the pasta in the boiling water and cook according to package instructions. Cook the mussels until they have all opened, about 3 minutes.

Drain the pasta well and toss into the pan with the mussels. Cook together for 30 seconds, add the parsley, toss well, and serve in a warm serving bowl.

BACCALÀ ALLA VESUVIANA

Salt Cod with Capers, Mint, and Chiles

2 pounds dried **salt cod,** (baccalà), as evenly thick as possible, soaked

6 tablespoons extra-virgin **olive oil**

1 medium **onion,** cut into ¼-inch dice

3 tablespoons **capers,** rinsed three times and drained

1 tablespoon hot red **pepper flakes**

1 28-ounce can **tomatoes,** juices drained and reserved, tomatoes crushed by hand

½ cup **dry white wine**

¼ cup chopped fresh **Italian parsley**

3 tablespoons fresh **mint** cut in thin ribbons

Serves 8

Cod that has been dried and salted, using a technique developed by Portuguese sailors in the 1500s, is a staple of the Italian holiday table. It is prepared in a number of ways, including braised with olive oil and white wine, batter-fried, and stewed in milk with onions and anchovies.

Buying salt cod is like buying olive oil: you generally get what you pay for. I recommend buying the thickest fillets in smaller portions with the bones removed. A consistent thickness makes the soaking process easier to time, as you need not adjust it for size variation. At markets in Italy the fishmongers soak the baccalà and sell it ready to cook.

NOTE: You need to soak the baccalà in 2 gallons of water in the refrigerator for 48 hours, changing the water at least twice a day, before you start this dish.

Drain the soaked baccalà and cut into 2-inch pieces; set aside.

In a 6- to 8-quart pot with sides at least 4 inches high, heat the oil until smoking. Add the onion, capers, and pepper flakes and cook over medium-low heat until soft and light golden brown, 8 to 10 minutes. Add the tomatoes, their juices, and the white wine and bring to a boil. Lower the heat and simmer for 20 minutes.

Add the baccalà pieces and simmer gently for 25 minutes, turning the fish once very carefully. Sprinkle with parsley and mint and serve warm or at room temperature.

GAMBERONI AL' ACQUA PAZZA

Shrimp in "Crazy Water"

6 tablespoons extra-virgin **olive oil**

1 medium **Spanish onion,** chopped into ½-inch dice

4 **garlic cloves,** thinly sliced

2 tablespoons chopped fresh hot **chiles**

1 **fennel** bulb, chopped into ½-inch dice, fronds reserved

1 28-ounce can **tomatoes,** crushed by hand, with juice

2 cups **dry white wine**

½ cup **sea water,** or ½ cup water mixed with 1 teaspoon sea salt

16 jumbo **shrimp,** peeled, heads and tails on

Freshly ground **black pepper**

Serves 4 to 8

Literally, "crazy water," the Southern Italian cooking liquid, is traditionally sea water and seasonings, although it has come to include tomatoes, hot peppers, and any number of additional ingredients.

Fresh shrimp is available every day in Amalfi, but even there the market is ruled by the blessings of the sea more than the whim or need of the cook. Flash-frozen shrimp from the Gulf of Mexico are a great product; buy those with the heads and shells still on and thaw them in the refrigerator overnight, as opposed to blasting the frozen block with water.

In a 6-quart soup pot, heat the oil over medium heat until smoking. Add the onion, garlic, chiles, and fennel and cook until soft and light golden brown, 8 to 10 minutes.

Add the tomatoes, wine, and water and bring to a boil. Lower the heat and simmer 10 minutes. Add the shrimp and simmer until cooked through, about 5 minutes. Pour into a soup tureen, garnish with fennel fronds, and serve with plenty of freshly ground black pepper.

ARAGOSTE ALLE BRACE

Grilled Lobster with Lemon Oil and Arugula

Anything tastes good when it's grilled and drizzled with this fragrant lemon oil. In Italy, giant scampi would be served this way, but here they are almost impossible to find and prohibitively expensive. Growing up in the Northwest, lobster always smacked of special occasion in my house, whereas Dungeness or king crab was standard Sunday fare during crab season.

LEMON OIL

1 cup extra-virgin **olive oil**

Juice and zest of 3 **lemons**

1 bunch fresh **marjoram,** tied tightly at stem end with a piece of string

3 tablespoons **limoncello** (page 110) or other lemon liqueur

4 2-pound live spiny or Maine **lobsters**

2 cups **arugula,** washed and spun dry

Pinch **coarse salt**

2 **lemons,** quartered lengthwise

Serves 4 to 8

Preheat the barbecue grill or broiler.

Combine the olive oil and lemon juice and zest in a small saucepan and place over medium heat. Bring to a near boil, remove from heat, and pour into a bowl. Immediately add the marjoram bunch and limoncello, cover, and steep like tea for 1 hour. (This oil can be stored in a covered jar away from light for up to a week.)

Kill lobsters by piercing the shells with a sharp point at the center of the back end of the eyes. Place the whole lobsters on the hottest part of the grill for 3 minutes per side and remove from the heat.

Cut the lobsters in half lengthwise and, careful not to lose a drop of the tomalley or roe, gently anoint them on the flesh side with the scented oil, using the marjoram bunch like a brush. Gently place them shell side down on the grill and cook until nearly done, 6 to 7 minutes. Turn the flesh side down and cook for 1 minute and remove to a platter.

Dress the arugula with 4 tablespoons of the scented oil and some coarse salt and pile in center of the platter with the lobster. Serve warm or at room temperature with any remaining oil and the lemon wedges on side.

CROCCANTE

Almond Brittle

¼ cup **almond oil**

4 cups blanched and sliced **almonds**

3 cups **sugar**

¼ cup **water**

Makes 1 pound

This hard and sweet brittle should be the next big thing imported from Italy, although it is so easy to make that there's no excuse for buying it. At the fancy pastry shops in Napoli it's often formed into little rafts or baskets and filled with tiny marzipan fruits or traditional Christmas cookies like those on pages 78–79. Once made, Croccante lasts indefinitely in an airtight cookie tin.

Preheat the oven to 400°F. Grease a cookie sheet with the almond oil. Place the almonds on a separate baking sheet and toast them until light golden brown, about 5 minutes. Set aside.

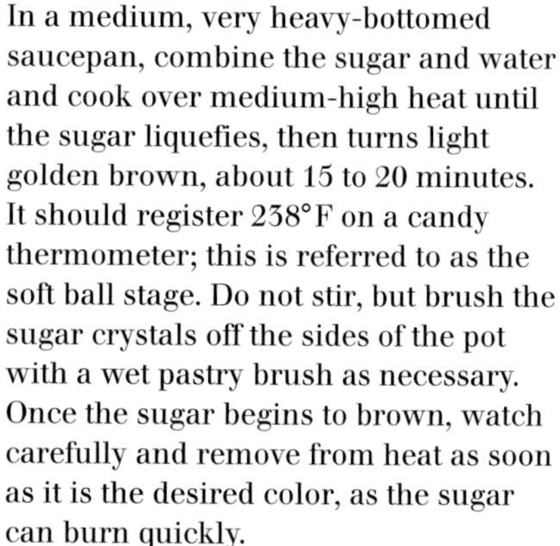

In a medium, very heavy-bottomed saucepan, combine the sugar and water and cook over medium-high heat until the sugar liquefies, then turns light golden brown, about 15 to 20 minutes. It should register 238°F on a candy thermometer; this is referred to as the soft ball stage. Do not stir, but brush the sugar crystals off the sides of the pot with a wet pastry brush as necessary. Once the sugar begins to brown, watch carefully and remove from heat as soon as it is the desired color, as the sugar can burn quickly.

Once the caramel is off the heat, immediately add the almonds to the pot and stir quickly to incorporate. Turn out onto the prepared cookie sheet, spreading quickly to an even thickness. Allow the brittle to cool completely, then break into festive shapes.

CANNOLI DI RICOTTA

Classic Cannoli

Good cannoli are truly hard to find in America, where the prestuffed tubes are inevitably soggy and the filling is made with inferior ricotta. If you can find good fresh ricotta at your local cheesemonger, and if you buy good candied citrus zest and if you stuff them only when you're ready to eat them, then you can enjoy a crisp and delicious cannolo. Skip any of these important details and you're doomed to disaster.

SHELLS

1½ cups all-purpose **flour**

¼ teaspoon ground **cinnamon**

1 teaspoon **granulated sugar**

1 teaspoon **unsweetened cocoa powder**

2 tablespoons unsalted **butter**

3 tablespoons **limoncello** (see page 110) or other lemon or orange liqueur

FILLING

16 ounces fresh sheep's milk or cow's milk **ricotta,** drained 1 hour in a cheesecloth-lined conical sieve

½ cup **superfine sugar**

1 tablespoon **vanilla extract**

4 tablespoons **candied orange zest**

¼ cup tiny **chocolate chips**

2 quarts **canola oil,** for frying

1 **egg white,** lightly beaten

Confectioners' sugar, for dusting (optional)

Makes 16 cannoli

You will need metal cannoli tubes to prepare this classic dessert correctly.

In a large bowl, whisk together the flour, cinnamon, sugar, and cocoa powder. Cut in the butter with two knives or a pastry cutter until the mixture resembles coarse crumbs. Add the limoncello, mix lightly, and shape the dough into a ball. Wrap the dough in plastic and refrigerate for 30 minutes.

In a mixing bowl, stir together the ricotta, sugar, vanilla, orange zest, and chocolate chips until well mixed. Spoon into a pastry bag with a ½-inch round tip and place in the refrigerator.

In a 3½-quart pot, heat the canola oil to 375° F.

Remove the dough from the refrigerator and divide into 4 pieces. Roll one piece with a rolling pin to a 1/16-inch thickness. Using a 4-inch cookie cutter, cut circles from the dough. Using the rolling pin, roll each circle into an oval and wrap each oval lengthwise around a metal form, sealing the point where they overlap with the beaten egg white. Flare the ends open with your fingers.

Gently drop the cannoli shells into the hot oil and fry until deep golden brown, 2 to 3 minutes. Remove from the oil with a slotted spoon and drain on paper towels. When the cannoli are cool enough to touch, twist the molds away from the shells. (The shells may be made one day in advance and allowed to rest, unfilled and uncovered.)

Use a pastry bag with a plain ½-inch round tip to fill the shells with the ricotta cream. Dust with confectioners' sugar if desired and serve immediately.

STRUFFOLI

Tiny Honey-Covered Fritters

3½ cups all-purpose **flour**

6 **egg yolks**

1 **egg**

Grated zest of 1 **lemon** and 1 **orange**

½ teaspoon **kosher salt**

1 tablespoon **limoncello** (see page 110)

4 cups **canola oil,** for frying

2 cups **honey**

Juice and zest of 1 **lemon**

Confectioners' sugar, for dusting

Candied orange or **lemon peel** or **sprinkles,** for garnish (optional)

Makes 50 to 60 fritters

These little fritters are the most beloved item on the Christmas table. Traditionally they are made several days before Christmas Eve and given to guests throughout the week, often presented in a golden horn of plenty made from bread dough. At my restaurant Babbo we place them on the center table so guests can help themselves on the way out.

In a mixer bowl, combine the flour, egg yolks, egg, zests, salt, and limoncello and mix well to form a firm dough, 8 to 10 minutes. Refrigerate for 30 minutes. When the dough has rested, remove from fridge and cut into golf ball-size pieces. Roll each golf ball into a ½-inch-thick dowel and cut each dowel into ½-inch pieces. Roll each piece between palms into a ball. Repeat with the remaining dough.

Heat the oil in a 12- to 14-inch skillet with at least 3-inch sides to 375°F. Drop balls in to cover about half of the surface of the oil and cook until dark golden brown. Use a spider or slotted spoon to turn them regularly; they will puff up while cooking. Remove when cooked to a tray covered with paper towels and drain well. This should make at least five batches, so be patient.

When all of the struffoli are cooked, heat the honey, lemon juice, and zest together in a wide 6- to 8-quart saucepan until quite warm, about 150°F, and substantially thinner. Add the struffoli and stir carefully until well coated. Remove from heat and allow to cool 5 minutes in the pan, stirring regularly. Pour out onto a large serving tray in the form of either a pyramid or a ring. Sprinkle with confectioners' sugar and any other choice of garnish. The struffoli should last a week or as long as your guests allow.

ZEPPOLE

Italian Doughnuts

These wonderful little fritters, along with sausage and peppers and braciole, are trademarks of the Italian street fairs held all over New York City. Unfortunately they are fried all day in the same, constantly darkening oil. This means that they're pretty good in the morning, but by the afternoon they're heavy and taste like old laundry. You should not have this problem at home and can even improve on the classic by serving them with a bit of warm jam for dipping.

2 cups **water**

1 teaspoon **kosher salt**

1 cup (2 sticks) unsalted **butter**

2 cups all-purpose **flour**

8 **eggs**

3 tablespoons **vanilla extract**

2 tablespoons plus 2 quarts **canola oil,** for frying

1 cup **confectioners' sugar**

1 cup best quality **strawberry jam**

Makes 20 to 24 little doughnuts

Place the water, salt, and butter in a 2-quart saucepan and bring to a boil. Have a whisk and a wooden spoon ready. Remove the pan from the heat and dump the flour in all at once, whisking it all in. Return to the burner and start stirring with a spoon. Cook, stirring constantly, until the dough starts to pull easily from the sides of the pan and forms a ball, about 3 minutes. Remove from the heat and stir until tepid, 6 to 8 minutes. Add the eggs, one at a time, stirring in each one completely before adding the next. Stir in the vanilla. Cool completely.

Line two cookie sheets with parchment and oil the paper with olive oil. Line another tray with several layers of paper towels. In a 4- to 6-quart pan, heat the oil to 375°F over medium heat. Place the dough into a pastry bag with a 1-inch round tip and pipe 2-inch rings onto the trays, as many as can fit. When all the dough is used, refrigerate the dough rings until chilled.

Using a spatula, slide the circles of dough into the hot oil, four or five at a time, and cook until golden brown, 3 to 4 minutes, carefully flipping to cook on the second side. Remove each batch as it is finished and drain on the paper towels. Sprinkle with confectioners' sugar while still hot.

Place the strawberry jam in a small saucepan and heat gently over medium heat. Serve the zeppole warm or at room temperature with the warm jam on the side.

GIFTS OF FOOD

Even though my restaurant staffs and I feed hundreds of people each day, I still love to send my friends and family gifts of homemade edibles or quaffables at the holidays. I put up jars of marinated olives, fruits, and vegetables, and prepare other food gifts just as families all over Italy do. There, foraged mushrooms are preserved throughout the autumn mushroom season and allowed to soak in a bath of oil and herbs for at least a month before serving. They are generally stored together with the wine, cheese, and salami—all homemade, all equally special—and only brought out for important meals or special guests.

Flavored olives is another favorite. Personalizing store-bought olives is the next best thing to curing them yourself, and is quite easy. Choose olives you like, cover with oil (or, for tangier olives, use half oil and half vinegar), stir in flavorings (see page 51), and allow to stand. The longer they bathe, the more pronounced their flavor will be.

It would not be an Italian Christmas without panettone. Italy's homage to the dreaded fruit cake is far lighter and has a higher cake-to-fruit ratio than its leaden counterpart.

Try one or all of these and you'll always have a pantry filled with good things to give and eat.

GRAPPA CHERRIES

4 cups **sugar**

3 cups **water**

3 pounds **cherries,** preferably Rainier, stems removed

1 liter **grappa**

Makes 4 quarts

In a large pot, stir together the sugar and water. Cook over medium heat until the mixture is clear, about five minutes. Remove from the heat and allow the mixture to cool.

Wash the cherries and dry with paper towels. Place them carefully in the four 1-quart jars, leaving one inch at the top of each jar. Fill the jars with equal amounts of grappa and sugar syrup. Close and seal the jars and store in a cool, dark place for at least 6 weeks before serving.

FUNGHI SOTT'OLIO

Marinated Mushrooms

I have called for readily available mushrooms, but feel free to substitute more exotic porcini, chanterelles, or hen of the woods. Serve at room temperature with grilled bread that's been rubbed with garlic.

1½ pounds **portobello mushrooms**

2 pounds **shiitake mushrooms**

1 pound **crimini mushrooms**

3 cups good **white wine vinegar**

1 bottle good **dry white wine**

4 fresh **bay leaves**

1 stem fresh **rosemary**

1 tablespoon hot red **pepper flakes**

19 **black peppercorns**

¼ cup **kosher salt**

4 to 6 cups extra-virgin **olive oil**

Makes 3 quarts

With a brush, clean the mushrooms of any dirt; do not wash. Cut the portobello caps into quarters and cut the stems into ½-inch-thick rectangles. Discard the stems from the shiitakes, leaving the caps whole. Halve the criminis.

Pour the vinegar and wine into a stainless steel 8-quart saucepan and add the bay leaves, rosemary, pepper flakes, peppercorns, and salt and bring to a boil. Add the mushrooms all at once, return to a boil, and cook over high heat for 20 minutes.

Drain the mushrooms in a colander, discarding the aromatics, then turn out onto a stack of kitchen towels to drain and dry well for about 30 minutes. Divide the mushrooms among three cleaned and sterilized quart jars with a couple of peppercorns and a pinch more pepper flakes in each jar. Fill each of the jars to the very top with oil and refrigerate overnight.

The mushrooms will absorb oil the first couple of nights, so it will be necessary to top up the oil after 3 or 4 days. Seal the jars with the caps and allow the mushrooms to marinate in the refrigerator for at least a week and up to 6 weeks.

PANETTONE

½ cup (1 stick) unsalted **butter,** softened

2 **eggs** and 3 **yolks**

3½ cups all-purpose **flour**

1 cup whole **milk**

1 cup **sugar**

½ cup **currants,** soaked in warm water for 1 hour and drained

Zest of 2 **oranges**

2 teaspoons **cream of tartar**

1½ teaspoons **baking soda**

Makes 1 cake, 12 slices

Preheat the oven to 425°F.

Butter and flour 8-inch tall round cake pan. In a mixer, cream the butter with the eggs and egg yolks until pale yellow, 3 to 4 minutes.

Replace the beater with the dough hook attachment, and with the mixer running, add half of the flour. Add half the milk and mix for one minute. Add the remaining flour followed by the remaining milk and all of the sugar and mix well. Continue mixing and kneading with the dough hook until the dough becomes dry enough to handle. Turn the dough out onto a floured surface and sprinkle with the currants, orange zest, cream of tartar, and baking soda. Knead by hand for 5 to 10 minutes.

Place the dough in the prepared pan and bake for 35 to 45 minutes, or until an inserted skewer comes out dry. The top should be quite cracked. Remove from the oven, invert onto a rack and cool. Slice into wedges to serve.

FLAVORED OLIVES

3 pounds **olives,** such as Gaeta, Sicilian, or Moroccan

FLAVORINGS (CHOOSE NO MORE THAN 3):

- 2 teaspoons **fennel seeds**
- 8 strips **orange zest**
- 2 teaspoons **toasted oregano**
- 2 to 4 dried **hot chiles,** crumbled
- 8 whole peeled **garlic cloves**
- 4 tablespoons **fresh herbs** such as thyme or rosemary

4 cups extra-virgin **olive oil** *or* 2 cups extra virgin **olive oil** and 2 cups **red vinegar**

Makes 6 pints

In a mixing bowl, gently toss the olives together with your preferred flavorings. Place the olives in 6 clean 1-pint jars and add enough olive oil (or half oil and half vinegar) to cover. Allow the olives to marinate in the refrigerate for at least 12 hours. Serve at room temperature.

CHRISTMAS

Christmas . . . that most magical and special time of the year. Family memories of the food we ate in this season are far clearer than of the gifts themselves, because the food was such a part of our traditions. Our house was the only one on the block where you could eat most of your gifts the moment you opened them: Grandma's cookie assortment and the inevitable box of clementines were as eagerly anticipated as a new toy. Our holiday season began just before Thanksgiving, with an official planning session. Then we'd head out to the "cut your own" ranch, where we'd argue the differences between blue spruce, Douglas fir, Scotch pine, and other trees before choosing our classic Christmas tree: very full, with a distinct triangular form from base to pinnacle and lots of branches. We'd spend an entire Saturday decorating the tree, dusting off the dried-cookie ornaments, the tinsel, and, most important, the lights. All this while giving our old (and even ancient) LPs by Johnny

DAY

APERITIVO

ACQUA D'ANANAS
Pineapple and Sweet White Vermouth

ANTIPASTI

SCAMORZA ALLA GRIGLIA
Grilled Smoked Mozzarella

CRESPELLE DI FORMAGGIO
Baked Crêpes Stuffed with Cheese

INSALATA DI RINFORZO
Pickled Vegetable Salad

PASTA

PERCIATELLI CON CACIO E UOVA
Spaghetti with a Hole, Sheep's Cheese, and Eggs

STRANGULAPRETI ALLA SORRENTINA
Gnocchi with Tomato Sauce and Mozzarella

SECONDI E CONTORNI

TACCHINO RIPIENO
Turkey Stuffed with Chestnuts and Prunes

SCAPECE DI ZUCCA
Marinated Butternut Squash

GATTO NAPOLETANO
Potato Cake

DOLCI

BABA
Yeast Cake Doused with Limoncello

ROCOCCO
Crisp Almond Rings

MUSTACIOLI
Iced Diamond Cookies

GRANDMA'S BISCOTTI
Twice-Baked Cookies

REGALI: GRANDMA'S COOKIE BOX
Fritelle al Miele; Divinity; No-Bake Chocolate Cookies; Snowdrops

Mathis, Bing Crosby, and my personal fave, Nat King Cole, a warm-up spin.

My brother, sister, and I always rose early on Christmas Day. We would open the gifts in order of age, with Gina, the youngest, first. Breakfast was generally something casual and sweet, like the cookies from Grandma or a panettone with coffee and juice, always finished with clementines, some no bigger than a mouthful.

We follow the same rhythm today. Dinner is served around 4, following the aperitivi. What a feeling of joy around the house. With Christmas music playing and Mom's goofy mechanical Santa dancing to "Jingle Bell Rock," the kids try to cool down from their frenzied pace. Everyone sits around the table to eat and the holiday spirit is served.

WINE RECOMMENDATIONS

As the family gathers on Christmas day, Biancolella Tenuta Frassitelli, D'Ambra Vini D'Ischia is opened freely. This lightly structured, aromatic wine makes for the perfect afternoon sipping. As the hearty antipasti of Christmas Day hit the table, a slightly chilled Mastro Rosso, Mastroberardino, with juicy fruit and notes of berry, drinks very easily and sets off the festivities with a bang. Serpico, Feudi Di San Gregorio is the way to headline the Christmas main event. This heavyweight will complement any braise or roast and linger in your guests' glasses until the cheese hits the table.

ACQUA D'ANANAS

Pineapple and Sweet White Vermouth

Chill martini glasses in the freezer until very cold. Place the pineapple in a blender with half of the vermouth. Blend until smooth and pour, over ice, into the martini glasses, garnish with sprigs of tarragon, top each glass with a splash of the remaining vermouth, and serve.

1 whole **pineapple** (2 pounds), peeled, cored, and cut into 2-inch chunks

1 fifth **sweet white vermouth**

1 bunch **tarragon** leaves

Serves 12

SCAMORZA ALLA GRIGLIA

Grilled Smoked Mozzarella

When making a dish as simple as this one, its success relies entirely on the quality of the ingredients. Scamorza is a cow's milk cheese, similar to mozzarella, that has been aged two weeks and smoked. Its name refers to its shape, which is similar to a dunce cap. If you cannot find a great scamorza or handmade smoked mozzarella, this dish will be a failure no matter how good you are in the kitchen. (My sources for great cheeses are on page 140.)

4 **scamorza,** or smoked **mozzarella,** 8 to 12 ounces each, cut in half

¼ cup best quality **sun-dried tomatoes,** chopped

½ cup **Olio Piccante**

1 bunch fresh **marjoram**

Serves 8

Preheat the grill and oil it with an oil-soaked towel. If you have no grill, a nonstick sauté pan will work in this case. Place the pieces of scamorza cut side down on the coolest part of the grill and cook until a dark golden brown skin forms, 5 to 6 minutes. Gently turn and repeat on the rounded side.

Remove to a platter and sprinkle each with a few shreds of sun-dried tomato, drizzle with a bit of spicy oil, and place the bunch of marjoram in the center of the plate, so guests can pinch a little onto their portions.

OLIO PICCANTE

Spicy Oil

2 cups extra-virgin **olive oil**

10 **jalapeño peppers,** coarsely chopped

1 cup hot red **pepper flakes**

2 tablespoons **sweet paprika**

Makes 2 cups

In a small saucepan, combine the oil, peppers, pepper flakes, and paprika. Heat to 170°F and simmer for 10 minutes. Remove from heat and allow to sit for 8 hours or overnight. Strain out solids and store up to 6 weeks in the refrigerator in a tightly covered jar.

CRESPELLE DI FORMAGGIO

Baked Crêpes Stuffed with Cheese

Crêpes make a big dinner easy because you can make them a month in advance and freeze them. The filling can be made the day before and refrigerated until the morning of the meal. These are delicious right out of the oven, but work quite well at room temperature, providing you don't use a commercial mozzarella, which becomes rubbery.

CRESPELLE

¾ cup all-purpose **flour**

2 **eggs**

¼ teaspoon **kosher salt**

1 cup whole **milk**

Olive oil, for pan

4 tablespoons (½ stick) melted unsalted **butter**

FILLING

2½ cups **ricotta**

1 pound fresh **mozzarella,** grated

1 cup freshly grated soft **sheep's milk cheese** (cacio, or a young provolone)

½ pound **sweet salami** or **soppressata,** cut into ⅛-inch dice

½ teaspoon freshly grated **nutmeg**

1 bunch **chives,** cut into long pieces

Makes about 18 crêpes; serves 6 to 10

First make the crespelle: Place the flour in a mixing bowl, add the eggs, and whisk them in. Add the salt, then whisk in the milk a little at a time until all the milk is incorporated. Allow the batter to stand for 20 minutes.

Preheat the oven to 450°F.

Heat a 6-inch nonstick pan over high heat until hot and brush with olive oil. Turn heat down to medium and pour 1½ tablespoons of batter into the pan. Cook until pale golden on the bottom, about 1 minute. Flip and cook just 5 or 10 seconds on the second side. Remove and set aside. Continue the process until all the batter has been used.

(The crêpes can be frozen for up to 2 months. Wrap stacks of up to 20 crêpes tightly in plastic and then in foil; when ready to use, thaw overnight in the refrigerator.)

Use 2 tablespoons of the melted butter to butter the bottom and all sides of a 10-by-8-inch ceramic baking dish. Combine the filling ingredients in a bowl; set aside ¼ cup. Fill each crespella with 3 tablespoons of the filling mixture and fold in half. Place in the baking dish. Repeat until the filling and crêpes are used, overlapping the crespelle in the dish.

Smear the reserved filling over the tops, drizzle with the remaining 2 tablespoons butter, and bake until piping hot and crispy on top, 12 to 15 minutes; some edges should look almost burnt. Remove and serve hot or at room temperature.

INSALATA DI RINFORZO

Pickled Vegetable Salad

4 tablespoons **kosher salt**

1 head **cauliflower**

3 cups **white wine vinegar**

1 teaspoon **fennel seeds**

4 **garlic cloves,** peeled and left whole

2 **carrots,** peeled and cut on the bias into ¼-inch-thick ovals

3 **celery stalks,** cut on the bias into ½-inch-thick pieces

16 **cipolline** (Italian baby onions), peeled and left whole

3 **red bell peppers,** seeds and stems discarded and cut into ½-inch-thick strips

1 **fennel bulb,** cut into ¼-inch batons

8 salt-packed **anchovies,** soaked, rinsed, and filleted (page 25)

18 **Gaeta olives,** pitted

18 large **green olives,** pitted

¼ cup **red wine vinegar**

½ cup extra-virgin **olive oil**

Kosher salt and freshly ground **black pepper**

½ cup **Italian parsley leaves**

Serves 8

The idea of this dish is to continuously replenish, or "reinforce," it over the course of several days. Every time vegetables are left over they are added to this constantly evolving salad. It is generally made on Christmas Eve, to serve on Christmas Day, and eaten through Epiphany, on January 6.

Place 4 quarts of water and 2 tablespoons of salt in a 6-quart pot and bring to a boil. Fill a large bowl with ice cubes and water. Cut the cauliflower into large florets and plunge into the boiling water. Cook until tender, 9 to 10 minutes. Remove with a slotted spoon and refresh in ice water, then set aside.

Pour out half of the boiling water (to leave about 2 quarts) and add the white wine vinegar, remaining salt, fennel seeds, and garlic and bring to a boil. Drop in the carrots, celery, cipolline, bell peppers, and fennel and cook until tender, 10 to 12 minutes. Drain in a colander, refresh in the ice bath, and drain again.

In a large mixing bowl, combine the cauliflower, cooked vegetables and garlic, the anchovies, both kinds of olives, the red wine vinegar, and the oil. Season with salt and pepper, toss well to mix, and arrange on a platter with the olives and anchovies near the top. Sprinkle with parsley and serve.

Pack any leftovers into a Mason jar, cover with a 50/50 mixture of olive oil and vinegar, and refrigerate until ready to serve again.

PERCIATELLI CON CACIO E UOVA

Spaghetti with a Hole, Sheep's Cheese, and Eggs

This simple dish is very similar to the Roman trattoria classic *spaghetti alla carbonara,* and makes a perfect early afternoon snack. If your guests have a problem with the egg yolks on top, help them stir the yolks in. The yolks will cook by the residual heat of the pasta and enrich this luscious and sensual dish.

½ cup extra-virgin **olive oil**

1 large **red onion,** cut into ¼-inch dice

1 pound **perciatelli** or **bucatini**

4 super-fresh **eggs** plus 1 **yolk** for each serving

Plenty of **kosher salt** and freshly ground **black pepper**

1 cup freshly grated **cacio cheese** (semisoft sheep's milk cheese)

¼ cup fresh **Italian parsley** cut into fine shreds

1 cup freshly grated **Parmigiano Reggiano**

Serves 4 to 8

Bring 8 quarts of water to a boil in a large pot and add 3 tablespoons salt.

In a 14- to 16-inch frying pan, heat the olive oil over medium heat till smoking. Add the onion and cook until soft and light golden brown, 7 to 9 minutes, and remove from heat. Drop the perciatelli into the boiling water and gently stir to separate. Cook until just short of al dente, following package instructions, and drain in a colander, reserving 1 cup of the cooking water. Pour the perciatelli into the frying pan with the onion and ½ cup of the reserved pasta cooking water and place over medium heat. Beat the whole eggs in a small bowl and season with salt and pepper. Add the eggs and cacio cheese to the pan and gently mix. Watch carefully, as you want them just to start to cook, but not scramble. The eggs will start to solidify after about 1 minute. Immediately remove the pan from the heat and add the Parmigiano and parsley. Pour into a warmed bowl, top with the whole yolks and more pepper, and serve immediately.

STRANGULAPRETI ALLA SORRENTINA

Gnocchi with Tomato Sauce and Mozzarella

GNOCCHI DOUGH

3 pounds **russet potatoes**

2 cups all-purpose **flour**

1 extra-large **egg**

Pinch of **kosher salt**

½ cup **olive oil**

CONDIMENT

1 teaspoon hot red **pepper flakes**

4 cups **Basic Tomato Sauce** (page 97)

Approximately 1 teaspoon **kosher salt,** or to taste

¼ cup fresh **basil leaves,** lightly packed

½ pound fresh **mozzarella di bufala,** cut into ¼-inch cubes

Serves 4 to 8

Who knows the true story behind these gnocchi's colorful name? Suffice it to say they are so irresistible even a priest could be tempted to gorge himself (the literal translation of *strangulapreti* is "priest stranglers.") The circumstances of a priest's demise aside, these are my family gnocchi and they are particularly tender.

Boil the whole potatoes until they are soft, about 45 minutes. While still warm, peel the potatoes and pass them through a food mill onto a clean pasta board.

Bring 6 quarts of water to a boil and set up an ice bath with 4 cups ice and 3 quarts water next to the stove.

Make a well in the center of the potatoes and sprinkle with the flour. Place the egg and salt in the center of the well and, using a fork, stir the egg into the flour and potatoes. Bring the dough together, kneading gently until a ball is formed and continue to knead gently another 4 minutes until the dough is dry to the touch. Cut a tennis ball–size hunk of dough off the main ball and roll it into a dowel about ¾ inch thick. Cut across the dowel to form pellets about 1 inch long. Flick each pellet down the tines of a fork to form the traditional gnocchi shape. Repeat with the remaining dough. Drop a third of the gnocchi into the boiling water. When they are floating aggressively (after 3 to 4 minutes of cooking), remove the gnocchi to the ice bath. Repeat with the 2 remaining batches of gnocchi and allow all gnocchi to cool in the ice bath. Drain the cooled gnocchi well, stir in the olive oil, cover, and refrigerate until ready to cook. The gnocchi will keep up to 36 hours in the fridge.

When you are ready to serve the gnocchi, bring 6 quarts of water to a boil and add 2 tablespoons salt. In a 14- to 16-inch fry pan, combine the pepper flakes, tomato sauce, and 1 teaspoon salt. Bring to a boil, reduce heat, and simmer 15 minutes, or until the sauce is as thick as a good porridge. (At this point the sauce could be refrigerated for up to 2 days.)

Drop the gnocchi into the boiling water and cook until floating aggressively, 4 to 5 minutes. Carefully transfer the gnocchi to the pan with the sauce, using a slotted spoon. Turn the heat to medium and toss gently for about 30 seconds. Tear the basil leaves into a few pieces and add to the sauce along with the mozzarella cubes. Toss together for 30 seconds longer, pour into a heated bowl, and serve immediately.

TACCHINO RIPIENO

Turkey Stuffed with Chestnuts and Prunes

1 whole **turkey breast,** boned, halved, and butterflied by your butcher, 5 to 6 pounds total

Kosher salt and freshly ground **black pepper**

3 tablespoons extra-virgin **olive oil,** plus ¼ cup

½ pound **pancetta,** cut into ½-inch pieces

1½ pounds ground **pork shoulder**

10 **prunes,** pitted and quartered

12 **chestnuts,** roasted, peeled, and halved

2 cups fresh **bread crumbs**

1 cup freshly grated **Parmigiano Reggiano**

2 **eggs**

2 tablespoons freshly ground **black pepper**

Freshly grated **nutmeg**

1 tablespoon each chopped fresh **rosemary** and **sage**

3 cups **dry white wine**

Serves 8 to 12

This is definitely my favorite way to do turkey because it never comes out dry. My wife, Susi, is always upset when she sees me prepare this abstract-looking sausage of a gobbler, but she's happy when she eats the tender and succulent meat and stuffing, all encased in a crisp and well-seasoned skin. The advantages of this method are twofold: it's in the oven only for an hour, freeing up cooking space for other dishes; and carving is simplicity itself—just cut straight through, like a regular roast. (Photograph page 66.)

Pound the butterflied breasts to flatten, then season with salt and pepper and refrigerate.

Preheat the oven to 400°F.

In a 12- to 14-inch sauté pan, heat 3 tablespoons of the oil over medium-high heat until smoking. Add the pancetta and cook until golden brown, 7 to 9 minutes. Add the pork and cook until it starts to brown in its own fat, about 25 minutes, stirring regularly. Drain all but 4 tablespoons of the fat from the pan and add the prunes and chestnuts. Continue cooking for 8 minutes, until the prunes really start to soften. Remove from the heat and allow to cool, about 20 minutes. Add the bread crumbs, Parmigiano, eggs, pepper, nutmeg, and herbs and just bring together, stirring with your hand. (Overmixing here can result in a lead torpedo for a stuffing, so don't do it.)

Place the two turkey pieces on a cutting board skin side down and divide the stuffing between them. Roll each of the breasts like a jellyroll and tie them firmly in several places with butcher's twine. Place the two rolls on a rack in a roasting pan, skin side up. Pour 2 cups of the wine over them, season with salt and pepper, and roast until dark golden brown outside and a meat thermometer reads 165° at the fattest part of the breast, about 1 hour, plus or minus 10 minutes. Remove and allow to rest 15 minutes before carving.

Add the remaining cup of wine to the roasting pan and deglaze, scraping with a wooden spoon. Cook for 5 minutes, then add the remaining ¼ cup of oil. Shake the pan to emulsify the sauce and season with salt and pepper.

Carve the roast into ½-inch slices and drizzle with the pan sauce.

SCAPECE DI ZUCCA

Marinated Butternut Squash

It is their simple way with seasonal vegetables that most amazes me about Italian cooks. This marinated squash dish is a lot more than the sum of its ingredients, for both flavor and presentation. You can make the whole dish in the morning; just hold the mint until the moment before serving.

As with almost all Italian vegetable dishes, a drizzle of your best extra-virgin olive oil, right before serving, will add infinitely to your pleasure. (Photograph page 66).

- 2 medium **butternut squash,** skin on, seeded and cut crosswise into 1-inch slices
- **Kosher salt** and freshly ground **black pepper**
- ½ cup extra-virgin **olive oil**
- ¼ cup **red wine vinegar**
- ½ medium **red onion,** sliced paper-thin
- ½ teaspoon hot red **pepper flakes**
- 1 tablespoon dried **oregano**
- 1 **garlic clove,** sliced paper-thin
- ¼ cup fresh **mint leaves**

Serves 8 to 12

Preheat the oven to 450°F.

Season the squash with salt and pepper, drizzle with ¼ cup of the olive oil, and arrange in a single layer on a cookie sheet or two. Roast until just tender, 18 to 20 minutes.

Meanwhile, stir together the remaining ¼ cup of oil, the vinegar, onion, pepper flakes, oregano, and garlic and season with salt and pepper.

When the squash is cooled, immediately transfer to a dish and pour the marinade over them. Allow to cool in the marinade for at least 20 minutes. This dish can be made up to 6 hours in advance but should not be refrigerated. Sprinkle with the mint just before serving at room temperature.

GATTO NAPOLETANO

Potato Cake

Not surprisingly, *gatto* refers to a cake—sweet or savory—deriving from the French *gateau.* I make this in a springform pan because it looks twice as cool as the classic pie-pan presentation. Like most of the contorno dishes in this book, it serves very well as a light lunch with a salad.

- 4 **eggs**
- ½ cup **whole milk**
- ¼ cup fresh **ricotta**
- 4 pounds **potatoes** (4 to 6 large)
- 1½ cups freshly grated **Parmigiano Reggiano**
- 1 cup freshly grated **pecorino cheese**
- ½ pound **soppressata** or **salami,** cut into 1-inch batons
- ¼ cup finely chopped **Italian parsley**
- 4 tablespoons (½ stick) unsalted **butter**
- ½ cup fresh **bread crumbs**
- 1 pound fresh **mozzarella,** cut into cubes, ¼ inch or smaller

Serves 8 to 12

Preheat the oven to 450°F.

In a medium bowl, lightly beat the eggs. Add the milk and ricotta and blend; set aside.

Boil the whole potatoes until tender, about 45 minutes. Drain and peel the potatoes and pass them through a food mill. While the potatoes are still warm, place them in a very large mixing bowl. Use a large rubber spatula to fold in the Parmigiano and pecorino, then add the soppressata and parsley and stir just enough to evenly mix. Gently stir in the egg mixture. (If you overstir now, the potato starch becomes tough and stringy later, so be careful.)

Butter a 12-inch springform pan with 2 tablespoons of the butter and dust with some of the bread crumbs. Plop half of the potato mixture into the pan and gently smooth it to the edges. Sprinkle the mozzarella over the potato mixture to within ½ inch of the outer edge, but not over. Top with the remaining potato mixture and carefully smooth over with a wet spatula. Sprinkle with remaining bread crumbs and dot with the remaining 2 tablespoons of butter. Bake the cake until light golden brown on top, 25 to 30 minutes. Remove from oven, let stand 15 minutes, unmold, and serve in wedges like a pie.

BABA

Yeast Cake Doused with Limoncello

In Amalfi these cakes are made small enough to fit into a soup spoon. In place of the more expected rum-flavored syrup, they are soaked in limoncello, the sweet lemon liqueur from the giant lemons of the Amalfi coast. A shop at the top of the Via Dei Mulini, near the town of Amalfi's lemon groves, sells baba from jars, all ready to eat.

CAKE

1 envelope active dry **yeast**

¼ cup warm **water**

2 tablespoons **cake flour** plus 4½ cups

6 tablespoons (¾ stick) unsalted **butter**

½ cup **sugar**

¼ teaspoon **kosher salt**

5 **eggs** plus 2 **yolks**

BATHING LIQUID

1 cup **water**

1 cup **sugar**

½ cup **limoncello** (see page 110) or other lemon or orange liqueur

2 cups **heavy cream**

Serves 8 to 10

Preheat the oven to 375°F. Butter then flour a 12-cup Bundt pan and set aside.

In a small mixing bowl, stir together the yeast and warm water until dissolved. Add 2 tablespoons of flour, stirring until a paste is formed. Set aside for 10 minutes. In a mixing bowl, beat the butter and sugar together until a ribbon forms when the beaters are lifted, 5 to 6 minutes. Place the dough hook attachment on the mixer. Add the yeast mixture, the remaining flour, the salt, and eggs and yolks to the butter mixture, and mix well, 10 to 15 minutes, until the dough pulls away from the sides of the bowl.

With floured hands, remove the dough from the mixing bowl in one piece. Place in the prepared pan, smoothing it into the ring shape. Cover with a towel and set in a warm spot to rise for 1 hour, until doubled. Bake the cake for 30 minutes until cooked through, or when a skewer inserted halfway in exits clean. Remove and allow to cool on a cake rack for 20 minutes. Remove the cake from the pan and place in a large bowl.

In a small saucepan, heat the water and sugar to boiling and stir to dissolve the sugar. Lower heat to a very high simmer and cook for 15 minutes to form a simple syrup. Remove from heat, stir in the limoncello, and allow to cool for 5 minutes. Poke the top of the cake all over with a thin knife to form 20 to 25 slender holes. Spoon the lemon syrup over the cake top and into holes. Pour off the syrup that drains out the bottom of the cake and repeat twice. Cool.

Whip the cream to soft peaks. Serve the baba with whipped cream piled high in the center hole.

ROCOCCO

Crisp Almond Rings

- 2 cups whole **almonds**
- $1\frac{7}{8}$ cups all-purpose **flour**
- $1\frac{3}{4}$ cups **sugar**
- Grated zests of 3 **oranges** and 3 **lemons**
- $\frac{1}{4}$ teaspoon freshly grated **nutmeg**
- $\frac{1}{4}$ teaspoon ground **cinnamon**
- $\frac{1}{4}$ teaspoon freshly ground **white pepper**
- $\frac{1}{4}$ teaspoon ground **cloves**
- 1 teaspoon **baking powder**
- $\frac{1}{2}$ teaspoon **baking soda**
- 1 cup **candied orange rind** cut in $\frac{1}{8}$-inch cubes (optional)
- Scant $\frac{1}{3}$ cup **water**
- 2 **eggs,** beaten

Makes 6 dozen cookies

Though a holiday standard, these doughnut-shaped cookies vary radically from town to town, particularly in their proportion of spices. I noticed that in Amalfi cloves are prominent, but in Salerno cinnamon is most distinct. This could also represent the variations among cooks and nothing more. Here grated nutmeg and white pepper add even more flavor and bite. (Photograph page 72.)

Preheat the oven to 350°F.

Place the almonds on a dry cookie sheet and toast in the oven until light golden brown, about 20 minutes, stirring occasionally. Remove and allow to cool. Roughly chop half the almonds by hand and process the other half to a powder in a food processor. Place both types of almonds into a mixing bowl and add the flour, sugar, orange and lemon zests, nutmeg, cinnamon, pepper, cloves, baking powder and soda, and candied orange if using; stir together. Add the water and mix until a homogeneous dough is formed. Cut 1-inch balls out of the dough and roll each ball on a lightly floured surface into a dowel 5 inches long. Join the ends of each dowel to form little circles and place on a greased cookie sheet. Brush with the beaten egg and bake until light golden brown, 10 to 12 minutes. Cool on the sheet for a minute or two before transferring to wire racks to finish cooling.

MUSTACIOLI

Iced Diamond Cookies

These dapper diamonds are required Christmas eating anywhere within a two-hundred-mile radius of Napoli. Each bakery, and certainly every nonna, contends his or her own is the "definitive" version; fortunately, this is a debate that no one could possibly lose—tasting every one could only be considered a victory. (Photograph page 72.)

DOUGH

3 cups all-purpose **flour**

1¼ cups **granulated sugar**

½ cup warm **water**

1 teaspoon **baking powder**

½ teaspoon **baking soda**

¼ teaspoon ground **cloves**

¼ teaspoon ground **cinnamon**

¼ teaspoon freshly grated **nutmeg**

Zest and juice of 1 **lemon**

½ teaspoon **vanilla extract**

ROYAL ICING

3 large **egg whites**

1 pound box **confectioners' sugar**

Pinch of **kosher salt**

3 tablespoons **unsweetened cocoa powder**

2 tablespoons warm **water**

Makes about 4 dozen cookies

Preheat the oven to 350°F.

In a mixing bowl, stir together the flour, sugar, water, baking powder and soda, spices, lemon juice and zest, and vanilla. Mix until the dough just comes together. Place on a lightly floured surface and knead until a smooth dough forms, about 2 minutes. Wrap in a kitchen towel and refrigerate for 20 minutes.

Roll out on a floured surface to ⅓ inch thick. Using a pizza wheel, cut the dough on the diagonal into 1-inch-wide strips. Cut through the strips on the diagonal again to form squat diamond shapes without wasting even a strip of dough. Place the shapes on an oiled cookie sheet, brush each with water, and bake for 14 minutes until light golden brown. Transfer to a wire rack and cool.

Make the icing: In an electric mixer, beat the egg whites with the confectioners' sugar on low speed until sugar is fully moistened, about 1 minute. Increase the speed to medium high and beat for 2 minutes, until glossy and smooth. Divide the mixture into two bowls. Add the cocoa to one of the bowls with the warm water, mix well, and set aside.

Pick up each cookie with tongs and dip it in the white icing so that half is coated, allowing the excess to drip back into the bowl. Repeat. Place on a wire rack to set, flat side down. When the cookies are dry, pick up one cookie with the tongs and dip the other side into the chocolate icing, just to the level of the white icing. Place again on the rack to set. These cookies can be stored up to a week in a parchment-lined cookie tin set in a cool place.

GRANDMA'S BISCOTTI

Twice-Baked Cookies

½ cup (1 stick) unsalted **butter,** softened

1½ cups **sugar**

3 **eggs**

¼ cup **heavy cream**

¼ teaspoon **anise oil**

1 teaspoon **anise seed**

3 cups sifted all-purpose **flour**

3 teaspoons **baking powder**

Makes 4 to 5 dozen cookies

These were the only biscotti I ever knew as a child, and so when the coffee bar craze hit in the late eighties and suddenly biscotti were a huge success, I was not caught by surprise. The sharp anise flavor in this recipe makes it a great dipper for remaining red wine after dinner, which, much to my real surprise having watched Grandma do this for years, is absolutely a killer.

Preheat the oven to 350°F.

In a mixer, cream together the butter and sugar. Add the eggs one at a time, waiting until each is incorporated before adding the next one. Add the cream, anise oil and seeds, the flour, and the baking powder and mix until a firm dough is formed.

Turn the dough out onto a work surface and form it into 2 logs approximately 24 inches long, adding more flour if needed for the logs to hold their shape. Place the logs on an ungreased cookie sheet and bake for 45 minutes, or until light golden brown.

Remove from the oven and while still warm slice each log diagonally into ¼-inch-thick slices. Return the slices to the cookie sheet cut side down and bake for 15 minutes more, turning after 7 or 8 minutes. Cool on wire racks. Store in an airtight container.

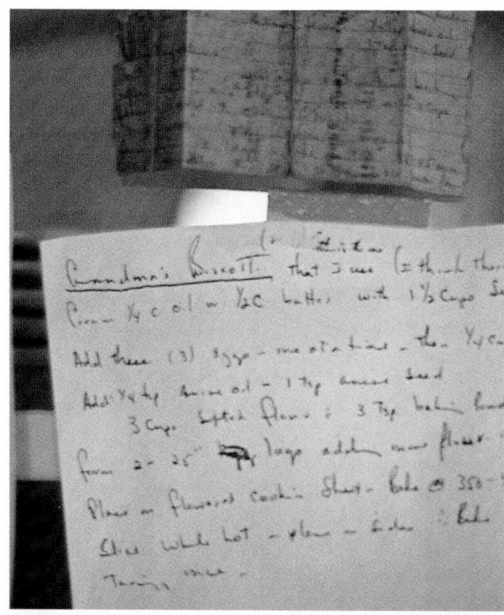

Grandma's
COOKIE BOX

My grandmother made many foods spectacularly well, but nothing I loved better than her Christmas cookies. Each year, about a week before Christmas, Grandma Batali's care package would arrive in the mail. (This continued all the way through college, when her gifts were even more devoutly appreciated.) It consisted of a box of clementines, a small present—usually socks or undies—and the big prize, a selection of her holiday cookies. Nestled in a shoebox, the cookies were stacked and arranged by type, each stack comforted by tissue paper. From the snickerdoodles to the *pizzelle,* the snowdrops to the biscotti, the ones with the silver dragees and the white-glazed Christmas trees, each one was special. At home they were placed under the tree and consumed at a leisurely pace; at school, they were finished within 5 minutes. Either way, they were appreciated immensely.

FRITELLE AL MIELE
FRIED DIAMONDS WITH HONEY

3 **eggs,** well beaten

1 tablespoon **granulated sugar**

1 teaspoon extra-virgin **olive oil**

½ teaspoon **vanilla extract**

3 cups all-purpose **flour**

Pinch of **kosher salt**

1 cup **olive oil,** for frying

½ cup **confectioners' sugar**

½ cup **honey**

Makes 3 to 4 dozen

Beat the eggs until they have large air bubbles but are still very wet. Add the sugar, oil, and vanilla and mix well. Add enough of the flour to make a soft dough.

On a floured work surface, roll the dough to ⅛-inch thickness and, with a knife or cookie cutter, cut diamond shapes that are 3 inches from point to point.

In a heavy-bottomed pot, heat the oil to 375°F. Drop the cookies in the oil and fry until golden brown, 3 to 4 minutes. Remove with a slotted spoon and allow to drain on a plate lined with paper towels. Sprinkle with the confectioners' sugar and drizzle with the honey.

DIVINITY

4 cups **sugar**

1 cup **light corn syrup**

¾ cup **water**

3 **egg whites**

1 teaspoon **vanilla extract**

1 cup chopped **walnuts**

Silver dragees (optional)

Makes 4 to 5 dozen

In a large saucepan, combine the sugar, corn syrup, and water and stir over low heat until the sugar is dissolved. Increase the heat and cook without stirring until the mixture reaches a temperature of 255°F. on a candy thermometer, or hard ball stage.

Meanwhile, in the bowl of an electric mixer, beat the egg whites until they form stiff peaks. When the sugar mixture reaches 255°F., add it to the whites in a fine stream, beating continuously, and beat for another 8 to 10 minutes, until the mixture loses its gloss and holds its shape. Stir in the vanilla and walnuts. Drop the mix by the teaspoonful onto a nonstick cookie sheet. Sprinkle with dragees if desired. When firm and cool store in an airtight container.

NO-BAKE CHOCOLATE COOKIES

2 cups **sugar**

½ cup **whole milk**

3 tablespoons **unsweetened cocoa powder**

¼ cup (½ stick) unsalted **butter**

3 cups **rolled oats**

1 cup **flaked coconut**

1 teaspoon **vanilla extract**

1 cup mini **marshmallows**

Makes 4 to 5 dozen

Line a cookie sheet with waxed paper and set aside.

In a large, heavy-bottomed saucepan, combine the sugar, milk, cocoa, and butter and stir to combine. Cook over high heat and bring to a boil. Allow to boil for 1½ minutes, remove from heat, then add the oats, coconut, vanilla, and marshmallows and stir well to combine. Drop by tablespoonfuls onto the prepared cookie sheet and chill.

SNOWDROPS

1 cup (2 sticks) unsalted **butter,** softened

½ cup **confectioners' sugar,** plus more for rolling cookies

1 teaspoon **vanilla extract**

2¼ cups sifted all-purpose **flour**

¼ teaspoon **kosher salt**

Makes 2 to 3 dozen

Preheat the oven to 400°F.

In a large bowl, combine the butter, confectioners' sugar, and vanilla and mix until well combined. Stir in the flour and salt until a firm dough is formed. Wrap the dough in plastic and chill in the refrigerator for 30 minutes.

On a lightly floured work surface, roll the dough into 1-inch balls. Place 1 inch apart on an ungreased cookie sheet, and bake until set but not browned, 10 to 12 minutes. Cool on sheets for a few minutes then roll in the confectioners' sugar.

NEW YEAR'S

EVE

I've always considered New Year's Eve an overrated holiday. The streets are filled with amateur drinkers on a hell-bent ride to drunkeness. For many, the evening is a fairy tale of black ties, carriages, and silver palaces; for me, it's about good food, better wine, and best friends. The only place I ring in the New Year is in the comfort of my home or the home of good friends. This is not to say the evening doesn't merit a bit of extra effort and a hint of excess in the menu and presentations. Some of the following recipes are simple, like the pizzette from Rita deRosa. Some are complex, like the timpano, inspired by Stanley Tucci's hilarious movie *Big Night*. All of these dishes are a little off the beaten path and have a certain air of the fantastic, in both presentation and preparation.

The end of a year is a great time to contemplate the year's achievements and difficulties, and for planning the next year in sober contemplation of our goals—for about a minute! I'd much rather spend my time celebrating the dance of life: the good, the bad, the silly, the mundane. It's about the elusive party of all that we breathe and see and sing

APERITIVO

TANGERINE, CAMPARI, AND SODA

ANTIPASTI

POLIPO ALLA LUCIANA
Octopus in the Style of the Prostitutes of Napoli

CROSTINI NAPOLETANI
Fresh Ricotta, Anchovy, and Oregano Toasts

MOZZARELLA IN CAROZZA
Fancy Grilled Cheese Sammies

PIZZETTE
Stuffed Ricotta Fritters from Rita deRosa

PASTA

SCIALATIELLI AI GAMBERETTI
Flat Pasta with Rock Shrimp and Zucchini

TIMPANO DI MACCHERONI
Mythic Pasta Dome

SECONDI E CONTORNI

COTECCHINO CON LENTICCHIE
Big Sausage with Lentils

BRACIOLONA
Braised Pork Roll with Ziti

PIZZE DI PATATE
Potato "Pizzas"

CIPOLLE RIPIENE
Stuffed Onions

SFORMATO DI CARDI
Cardoon Custard

DOLCI

AFFOGATO AL CAFFE
Coffee Semifreddo "Drowned" in Coffee

SANGUINACCIO
Cinnamon Chocolate Pudding with Pine Nuts

PIZZELLE
Thin Waffle Cookies

REGALI: AFTER-DINNER DRINKS
Digestivi, Caffé, Flavored Grappas

and rejoice, and the truest gift is to appreciate even a tenth of that delicious circus. So when it is the new year, celebrate it with joy, celebrate your things you're happiest with, celebrate your family, the friends and the food, but most of all, celebrate well.

WINE RECOMMENDATIONS

As friends begin to gather, nibbling on Mozzarella in Carozza and Pizza di patate, offer a bright sparkler like Kalimera Brut Dell'Isola D'Ischia. Although sparkling wines are not common in the south, Kalimera is a perfect specimen, with a light, crisp citrus flavor that is not overbearing on the palate. Traditional New Year's dishes need a wine with structure and importance that can stand up to their earthy flavors; Campanaro, Feudi Di San Gregorio, a white blend of Fiano and Greco, is made to stand alone and deliver. Its extreme ripe style gives it the palate weight to stand up to flavor with a finesse that allows serious contemplation. And because big events command important wines, end with a Silvia Imparato Montevetrano. This is by most accounts one of the most important Italian wines of the last ten years. Made of Cabernet Sauvignon, Merlot, and Aglianico, this massive red wine will leave your guests cooing. As the evening winds down and only your closest friends remain, settle your stomachs and greet the morning with fortified sweet Aglianico, Irpinia Aantheres Liquoroso, Mastroberardino. This sipping liquor will first appear as an amaro, then slowly evolve into a port that coats your palate and warms the stomach.

TANGERINE, CAMPARI, AND SODA

14 **tangerines**

1 quart **soda water**

8 ounces **Campari**

Serves 8

Juice 12 of the tangerines and chill the juice. Cut the remaining 2 tangerines into ⅛-inch slices. Fill 8 highball glasses with ice and place 2 tangerine slices in each glass. Add 3 ounces of juice to each glass and fill the glass to ⅔ full with soda. Pour in Campari to fill the glass and float one more tangerine slice in each glass.

POLIPO ALLA LUCIANA

Octopus in the Style of the Prostitutes of Napoli

1 **octopus,** about 3½ pounds, or an equal weight of smaller ones

3 tablespoons **red wine vinegar**

1 **wine cork**

10 tablespoons extra-virgin **olive oil**

4 **garlic cloves,** peeled and left whole

1 tablespoon hot red **pepper flakes**

2 cups **Basic Tomato Sauce** (page 97)

½ cup **dry white wine**

Kosher salt and freshly ground **black pepper**

¼ cup finely chopped **Italian parsley**

Serves 8

The best technique for tenderizing octopus is the subject of infinite debate. Some beat it on a rock, others insist it must cook in its own juices, while others believe that it should be cooked only in the water of its birthplace. I've tried lots of methods, but the one that yields the best results is cooking it in lots of simmering water with a wine cork. This produces juicy, tender flesh that most resembles the octopus in its natural state. Cooking it without the cork will eventually yield a tender beast but at the cost of ravaged tentacles.

In a 2-gallon pot place the octopus, vinegar, and the cork. Fill the pot with water, bring to a boil, then lower the heat and simmer until the octopus is tender, 50 to 60 minutes. Drain the octopus, allow to cool, and cut into bite-size pieces. Use the entire octopus including the head, except for the beak and eyes, which should be given to the cat.

In a 6-quart saucepan, heat 6 tablespoons of the oil until smoking. Add the garlic and the pepper flakes and cook until light golden brown, 4 to 5 minutes. Add the tomato sauce, the wine and the octopus pieces, and bring to a boil. Lower the heat and simmer for 25 to 30 minutes.

Adjust the seasoning and stir in the parsley and remaining 4 tablespoons of oil. Serve immediately, or allow to cool and serve at room temperature.

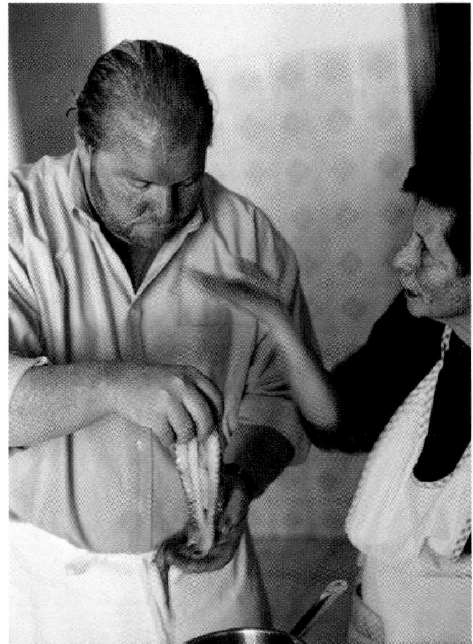

CROSTINI NAPOLETANI

Fresh Ricotta, Anchovy, and Oregano Toasts

Crostini refers to a whole family of antipasti based on thin slices of bread, toasted, sometimes brushed with olive oil, and covered with any number of savory toppings.

If you can, buy fresh anchovies and marinate them yourself or buy them already marinated from an Italian or Hispanic deli (where they are known as *alici marinati* or *boquerones* respectively; see Note page 25).

- 1 **baguette,** cut into 16 slices, or 8 slices country bread
- 3 **garlic cloves,** peeled and left whole
- 2 cups fresh **ricotta**
- 2 tablespoons freshly ground **black pepper**
- 3 tablespoons chopped fresh **oregano**
- 16 **anchovy fillets,** preferably marinated fresh fillets (see page 22)
- 3 tablespoons extra-virgin **olive oil**

Serves 4 to 8

Preheat the broiler. Place the bread slices on a baking sheet and toast until light golden brown on both sides. While still hot, rub each slice with a garlic clove to impart a delicate flavor.

In a bowl, mix the ricotta, black pepper, and oregano and smear casually over each bread slice. Top each with an anchovy fillet and return to the cookie sheet. Broil until cheese just oozes, about a minute. Arrange on a serving platter, drizzle with olive oil, and serve.

MOZZARELLA IN CAROZZA

Fancy Grilled Cheese Sammies

These spiffy sandwiches really capture the essence of a New Year's celebration because they're easy and elegant. Their entire success rests on the quality of the main event, the mozzarella. To really sex them up, allow the individual sammies to soak up a good amount of the egg mixture so they really ooze richness.

8 slices American-style **sandwich bread,** crusts removed

1 pound fresh **mozzarella di bufala,** cut into four 3-by-4-inch slices

4 **eggs** plus 3 **yolks**

1 cup whole **milk**

1 teaspoon chopped fresh **thyme leaves**

1 teaspoon **kosher salt**

2 tablespoons extra-virgin **olive oil**

2 tablespoons unsalted **butter**

Serves 4 to 8

Top each of 4 slices of bread with a piece of mozzarella. Cover with the 4 remaining slices of bread to form sandwiches. Trim the bread to within ¼ inch of the cheese and set aside.

In a wide, shallow bowl, whisk the eggs and the yolks together. Add the milk, thyme, and salt and mix until well blended. Dip the sandwiches into the egg mixture one by one to coat, and set aside.

In a 12- to 14-inch nonstick sauté pan, heat 1 tablespoon of the olive oil until smoking. Add 1 tablespoon of the butter and cook over medium-high heat until the sizzling subsides. Place 2 sandwiches in the pan and cook slowly until golden brown on the first side, about 2 minutes. Flip each sandwich and cook on the other side for 2 more minutes. Remove sandwiches and set aside in a warm oven. Repeat the process with the remaining oil, butter, and sandwiches. Serve immediately.

PIZZETTE

Stuffed Ricotta Fritters from Rita deRosa

DOUGH

1 ounce active dry **yeast**

¼ cup warm **water**

3¾ cups all-purpose **flour**

½ cup (1 stick) unsalted **butter,** softened

3 **eggs**

1 teaspoon **kosher salt**

FILLING

½ cup **smoked mozzarella** cut into ¼-inch dice

½ cup **salami** cut into ¼-inch dice

½ cup good **ricotta**

1 **egg**

¼ cup freshly grated **Parmigiano Reggiano**

2 cups extra-virgin **olive oil,** for frying

Makes 30 to 35 pizzette; serves 8 to 10

Similar to calzones, pizzette are small, fried dough pockets filled with a mixture of cheese and cured meats. I was introduced to these delicious little snacks by Maurizio, Franco, and Rita deRosa, whose restaurant Pierino was a passionate tribute to the cooking and winemaking of Campania. Though the restaurant has since closed, I was fortunate enough to become friends with the deRosas, who introduced me to an entire world of flavor, regional distinctions, and the true heart of Napoli.

Mix the yeast in a small measuring cup with the warm water and let stand for 2 minutes. Mound the flour on a board as if for making pasta, add the butter and mix with your fingers until cut into the flour. Remake the well, add the eggs, the salt, and the yeast mixture and mix until a firm dough has formed, about 5 minutes. Cover with a dish towel, and allow to rest 10 minutes.

Meanwhile, make the filling: In a mixing bowl, stir together the smoked mozzarella, salami, ricotta, egg, and Parmigiano until well mixed and set aside.

Cut the dough into quarters and roll each quarter on a smooth cutting board to a ¹⁄₁₆th-inch thickness. Using a water glass or pastry cutter, cut the dough into 3-inch circles. Place 1 tablespoon of the ricotta mixture in the center of each circle and fold the dough over to form a half-moon. Pinch the edges together to seal. Let the formed pizzette rest for 15 minutes in a warm part of the kitchen. Meanwhile, heat the oil in a tall-sided pan to 375°F. Drop in three or four of the pizzette and fry until light golden brown, about 4 minutes, turning after about 2 minutes. Transfer the cooked pizzette to a tray lined with paper towels and keep warm in a 200°F oven while you fry the remaining pizzette. Serve hot.

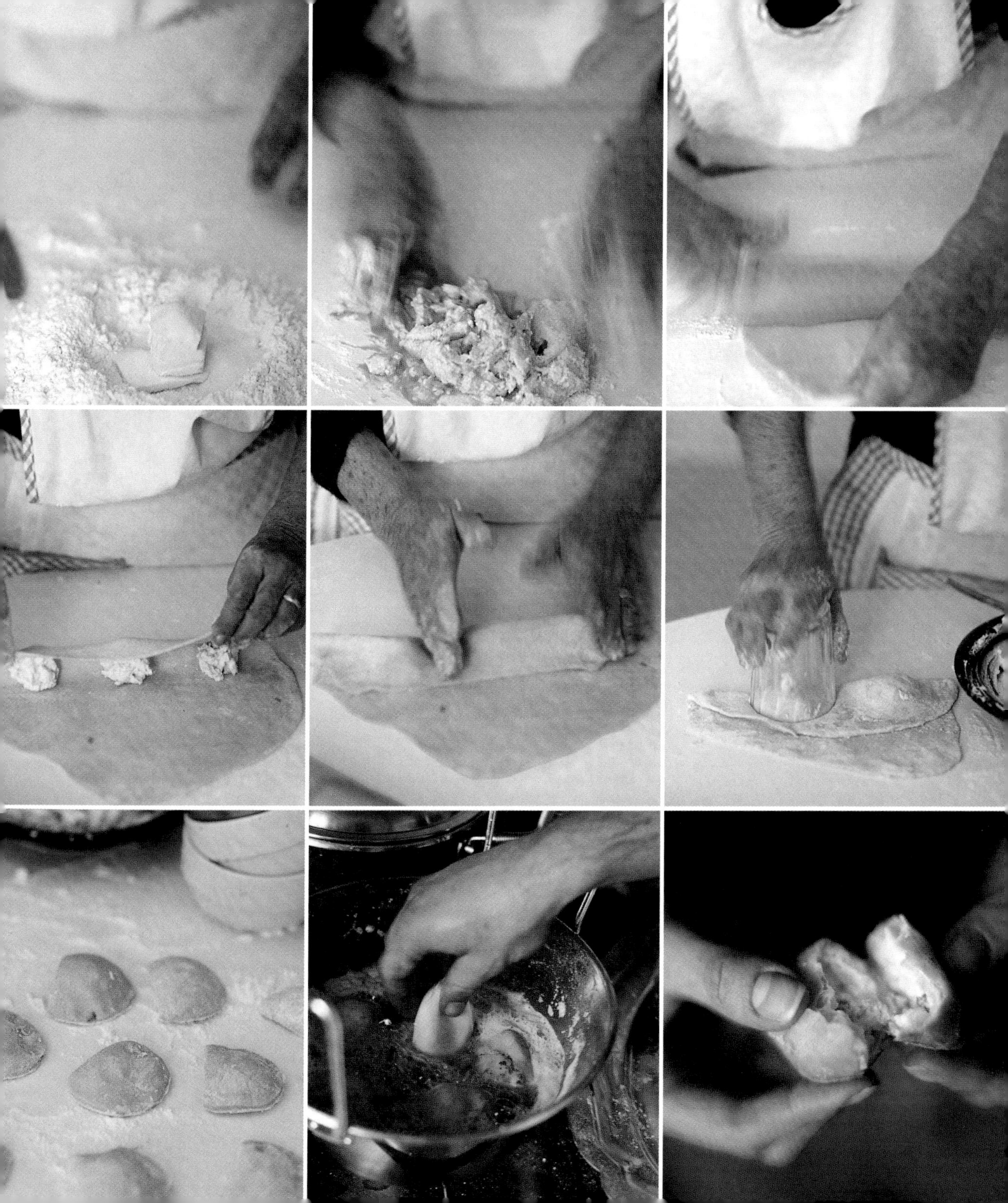

SCIALATIELLI AI GAMBERETTI

Flat Pasta with Rock Shrimp and Zucchini

These incredible noodles were the highlight of a fabulous dinner in an Amalfitano restaurant called La Caravela, part of a serious dining trip that I shared with my partners at Esca and the famous photographer Quentin Bacon. The chef begrudgingly parted with this recipe at the end of a spectacular series of dishes, each more interesting than the last. The dough is a little tricky in its stickiness, but the pasta's truly original texture is well worth the effort.

DOUGH

2 bunches **basil**

4 cups **cake flour**

2 **eggs**

1 cup whole **milk**

¼ cup freshly grated **pecorino cheese**

CONDIMENT

10 tablespoons extra-virgin **olive oil**

6 **garlic cloves,** thinly sliced

1 medium **zucchini,** cut into ¼-inch-thick half-moons (about 1 cup)

1 teaspoon hot red **pepper flakes**

2 cups **dry white wine**

4 tablespoons (½ stick) unsalted **butter**

1 pound **rock shrimp** or medium shrimp, peeled

¼ cup finely chopped **Italian parsley**

Freshly ground **black pepper**

Serves 4 to 8

Bring a pot of water to a boil and fill a bowl with ice cubes and water. Blanch the basil in the boiling water for 10 seconds, then refresh in the ice water. Drain and chop finely; you should have ¼ cup. Make a mound of the flour, then make a well in the center. Crack the eggs into the well, pour the milk over, and add the basil. Using a fork, stir the egg mixture slowly into the flour to form a wet dough. Add the grated cheese and, working now with your hands, bring the dough together and knead 8 to 10 minutes to form a smooth dough. Allow to rest 15 minutes covered in plastic wrap.

Set up a pasta rolling machine and cut off a piece of pasta dough the size of a tennis ball. Roll the pasta through the rollers on the widest setting, then fold it by thirds and run it through again on the same setting. Repeat this three times, being careful to add very little flour, as it will dry out the pasta. Run the pasta through the next two thinner settings. It should be quite thick.

Lay the sheet of pasta onto a floured cutting board and use a knife to cut crosswise into ⅓-inch strips. Lay the cut noodles on a kitchen towel and cover with another. Roll and cut the remaining pasta the same way.

Bring 6 quarts of water to a boil and add 2 tablespoons of salt. In a 12- to 14-inch sauté pan, heat 6 tablespoons of the oil and the garlic over medium heat until the garlic is light golden brown, 2 to 3 minutes. Add the zucchini pieces and cook until just soft, 2 to 3 minutes. Add the pepper flakes, wine, and butter, bring to a boil, and cook for 1 minute. Add the shrimp and remove from the heat.

Drop the pasta into the boiling water and cook until tender yet al dente, about 3 minutes. Drain and toss into the pan with the shrimp and place pan over high heat. Cook until the shrimp are just cooked through, about a minute, and pasta and sauce have become one.

Add the parsley and toss through with the remaining 4 tablespoons of oil, off the heat. Pour into a heated bowl and serve with plenty of pepper.

TIMPANO DI MACCHERONI

Mythic Pasta Dome

DOUGH

2½ cups all-purpose **flour**

6 ounces **lard,** butter, or vegetable shortening

4 **egg yolks**

½ teaspoon **kosher salt**

2 tablespoons unsalted **butter**

1½ cups toasted **bread crumbs**

2 pounds **rigatoni** or **ziti**

2 tablespoons extra-virgin **olive oil**

FOR THE ASSEMBLY

1 recipe **Ragù Napoletano** (page 96)

2 cups freshly grated **Parmigiano Reggiano**

1 recipe **Besciamella Sauce** (page 96)

½ pound **prosciutto crudo** cut into ¼-inch dice

Several gratings of **nutmeg**

1 recipe **Polpette alla Napoletana** (page 97)

Serves 8

Anyone who has seen Stanley Tucci's cinematic masterpiece, *Big Night,* will remember Primo's rendition of this classic, which takes its name from a large drum. My version differs from that one in many ways, but like it, it makes for a dramatic presentation. Surprisingly, it is not nearly as tricky to prepare as it looks. Except for the rigatoni you can prepare the whole thing the day before; just blanch the pasta and assemble the dish in the afternoon before your guests arrive. It can then rest in the refrigerator for several hours before the final cooking. You will need a 4-quart metal mixing bowl for the final assembly.

Place the flour on a wooden work surface and make a well in the top. Cut the lard into ¼-inch pieces and place in the center of the well with the yolks, ½ teaspoon salt, and a teaspoon of ice water. Mix well with the tips of your fingers to form a lumpy mass. Bring together as a dough and knead for 4 to 5 minutes. Wrap in plastic and set aside.

Preheat the oven to 375°F. Bring 6 quarts of water to a boil in a spaghetti pot and add 2 tablespoons of salt.

Roll out the pasta to a large circle ¼ inch thick. Butter the metal bowl and dust with the bread crumbs. Lay the pasta in the bowl to line it completely, with a 1½-inch edge hanging over the rim.

Cook the rigatoni in the boiling water, cooking 3 minutes less than the package instructions direct. Drain and refresh under cold running water until cold, 2 to 3 minutes. Toss with the olive oil and set aside.

Mix half of the cooked rigatoni with 2½ cups meat sauce and ½ cup of Parmigiano and set aside. Mix the remaining cooked rigatoni with half of the Besciamella, ¼ cup of Parmigiano, the prosciutto, and nutmeg. Place the creamed rigatoni into the bowl and press lightly. Sprinkle with more grated Parmigiano. Arrange the meatballs on top in an even layer and press down carefully. Sprinkle with more Parmigiano. Spread the meat-sauced pasta over the meatballs and press down gently.

Fold the extra pasta over the whole thing and press gently. Cover the open top with foil and bake for 1 hour 20 minutes.

Remove from the oven, remove the foil, and invert onto a large serving platter without removing the bowl. Allow to rest 10 minutes, then carefully loosen the pasta around the sides with a knife and knock with your knuckles to release the bowl. Serve immediately with the remaining Parmigiano on the side, cutting the timpano into wedges.

RAGU NAPOLETANO

Neapolitan Meat Sauce

¼ cup extra-virgin **olive oil**

½ pound boneless **veal shoulder,** cut into chunks

½ pound boneless **beef chuck,** cut into chunks

Kosher salt and freshly ground **black pepper**

1 **onion,** finely chopped

¾ cup **dry red wine**

2 28-ounce cans peeled **plum tomatoes** and juice, passed through a food mill

½ pound **sweet Italian sausages**

Pinch of hot red **pepper flakes**

Makes 3 quarts

In a large pasta pot or Dutch oven, heat the oil until smoking. Season the veal and beef with salt and pepper to taste and sear 5 or 6 pieces at a time over medium heat until dark golden brown. Remove to a plate and repeat with the remaining meat chunks.

Add the onion to the pan and sauté, scraping the pan with a wooden spoon to loosen any brown bits. Cook until the onions are golden brown and very soft, 10 minutes. Add the wine, browned meat chunks, tomatoes, sausages, and pepper flakes and bring to a boil.

Reduce the heat to a simmer and cook 2½ to 3 hours, stirring occasionally and skimming off the fat as necessary.

Remove from the heat and remove meat and sausages from sauce. Cover well and save for another meal. Adjust seasoning with salt and pepper and allow to cool.

BESCIAMELLA SAUCE

5 tablespoons unsalted **butter**

¼ cup all-purpose **flour**

3 cups whole **milk**

2 teaspoons **kosher salt**

½ teaspoon freshly grated **nutmeg**

Makes 3¼ cups

In a medium saucepan, heat the butter until melted. Add the flour and stir until smooth. Cook over medium heat until light golden brown, 6 to 7 minutes.

Meanwhile, heat the milk in a separate pan until just about to boil. Add the milk to the butter mixture 1 cup at a time, whisking continuously until very smooth. Bring to a boil and cook for 30 seconds. Remove from heat and season with salt and nutmeg.

POLPETTE ALLA NAPOLETANA

Neapolitan Meatballs

3 cups day-old **bread** cut into 1-inch cubes

1¼ pounds **ground beef**

3 **eggs,** beaten

3 **garlic cloves,** minced

¾ cup grated **pecorino cheese**

¼ cup finely chopped **Italian parsley**

¼ cup **pine nuts,** baked for 8 minutes in a 400° F. oven

½ teaspoon **kosher salt**

½ teaspoon freshly ground **black pepper**

¼ cup extra-virgin **olive oil**

2½ cups **Basic Tomato Sauce** (see box)

Makes 12 to 15 meatballs

In a shallow bowl, soak the bread cubes in water to cover for a minute or two. Drain the bread cubes and squeeze with your fingers to press out the excess moisture.

In a large bowl, combine the bread cubes, beef, eggs, garlic, pecorino, parsley, toasted pine nuts, salt, and pepper and mix with your hands to incorporate. With wet hands, form the mixture into 12 to 15 meatballs, each smaller than a tennis ball but larger than a golf ball.

In a large, heavy-bottomed skillet, heat the oil over medium heat until almost smoking. Add the meatballs and, working in batches if necessary to avoid overcrowding the pan, cook until deep golden brown on all sides, about 10 minutes. Add the tomato sauce and reduce the heat to a simmer. Cook all the meatballs for 30 minutes. Set aside and allow to cool; save the sauce for another use.

BASIC TOMATO SAUCE

¼ cup extra-virgin **olive oil**

1 large **onion,** cut in ¼-inch dice

4 **garlic cloves,** thinly sliced

3 tablespoons chopped fresh **thyme** leaves, or 1 tablespoon dried

½ medium **carrot,** finely shredded

2 28-ounce cans **peeled whole tomatoes,** crushed by hand and juices reserved

Kosher salt to taste

Makes 4 cups

In a 3-quart saucepan, heat the olive oil over medium heat. Add the onion and garlic and cook until soft and light golden brown, 8 to 10 minutes. Add the thyme and carrot and cook 5 minutes more, until the carrot is quite soft. Add the tomatoes and juice and bring to a boil, stirring often. Lower the heat and simmer for 30 minutes until as thick as hot cereal. Season with salt. This sauce holds 1 week in the refrigerator or up to 6 months in the freezer.

COTECCHINO CON LENTICCHIE

Big Sausage with Lentils

1 tablespoon **kosher salt**

8 ounces **brown lentils**

1 medium **carrot,** peeled and cut into ¼-inch dice

2 **garlic cloves**, thinly sliced

12 fresh **sage leaves**

¼ cup extra-virgin **olive oil**

¼ cup **red wine vinegar**

Kosher salt and freshly ground **black pepper**

2 **cotecchino sausages,** about 2 pounds each (see Source List, page 140)

Serves 8

It wouldn't be New Year's in Italy without lentils and sausage. Their round shapes suggest coins, symbolizing the riches and good luck that will follow in the new year. Cotecchino, a large fresh pork sausage, is most typical of the Emilia-Romagna region, but is embraced throughout Italy at this festive time.

Bring 6 cups of water to a boil and add the salt. Add the lentils, carrots, garlic, and sage and boil until the lentils are tender yet firm, about 25 minutes. Drain and place in a mixing bowl. Add the oil and vinegar, season with salt and pepper, and mix well. Set aside.

Prick the sausages with a pin several times. Place in a large pot of cold water and bring to a boil over medium heat. Reduce the heat to a very low boil and cover the pot. Cook for 1½ hours.

Place the marinated lentils on a large serving platter to form a bed for the cotecchino. Drain the sausages and cut into ¼-inch rounds. Arrange the sausage on the lentils and serve hot or at room temperature.

BRACIOLONA

Braised Pork Roll with Ziti

The most difficult part of this truly spectacular dish may be finding a piece of pork big enough to stuff and roll. Few supermarkets stock a piece of pork shoulder this large, and you will probably need to special-order it. This is when it definitely pays to have a good relationship with a local butcher. The sauce from this dish is generally used to dress ziti, which is served as a pasta course. The meat is held in a warm place and served as a secondo, or main course.

3 pounds boneless **pork shoulder** or leg, butterflied and pounded to yield 1 large piece ½ inch thick and 12 inches square

Kosher salt and freshly ground **black pepper**

½ cup finely chopped **Italian parsley** plus 2 tablespoons

¼ cup **pine nuts,** baked for 8 minutes in a 400° F. oven

½ cup dried **currants**

¾ cup freshly grated young **pecorino** cheese

16 slices **prosciutto di Parma,** about ½ pound

4 hard-boiled **eggs,** peeled and quartered lengthwise

Several gratings of **nutmeg**

4 tablespoons dried **oregano**

¼ cup extra-virgin **olive oil**

2 **red onions,** cut into ¼-inch dice

4 **garlic cloves,** thinly sliced

2 cups **dry white wine**

3 28-ounce cans **plum tomatoes,** crushed by hand, juices included

2 teaspoons hot red **pepper flakes**

2 pounds **ziti,** cooked until al dente (optional)

Serves 8

Lay the pork on a cutting board and season with salt and pepper. In a mixing bowl, stir together ½ cup of the parsley, the pine nuts, currants, and ½ cup of the pecorino and season with salt and pepper. Lay the prosciutto slices over the pork piece to cover completely. Sprinkle the parsley mixture evenly over the prosciutto. Arrange the eggs in two rows across the meat. Grate nutmeg over the entire piece and sprinkle with 2 tablespoons of the oregano, rubbing it between your fingers to release the essential oils. Carefully roll the piece up like a jellyroll and tie firmly with butcher twine in several places. Season the roll with salt and pepper. (The tied roll can be refrigerated for a day or two.)

In an 8-quart Dutch oven, heat the oil until smoking. Carefully brown the pork roll on all sides, taking your time to get a deep golden brown; this should take 15 to 20 minutes. Remove the meat and set aside.

Add the onions, remaining 2 tablespoons of oregano, and the garlic to the pan and cook until light golden brown and soft, 9 to 11 minutes. Add the wine, tomatoes, and pepper flakes and bring to a boil. Return the pork to the pan and simmer partially covered for 1 hour 20 minutes, moving occasionally to avoid sticking.

Transfer the pork to a cutting board and remove the butcher twine carefully. Slice the braciolona ¾ inch thick with a very sharp knife. Arrange like shingles on a warm platter and sprinkle with the remaining ¼ cups of grated pecorino and remaining chopped parsley. Cover and keep warm if serving after the pasta course.

PIZZE DI PATATE

Potato "Pizzas"

4 pounds **russet potatoes**

1½ cups **ricotta**

1 cup freshly grated hard **provolone cheese**

2 **eggs**

½ cup finely chopped **Italian parsley**

Kosher salt and freshly ground **black pepper**

2 cups fresh **bread crumbs**

½ cup extra-virgin **olive oil**

Serves 8

Not really pizza, these little spud pies are usually as large as a real Neapolitan pizza, 13 to 14 inches across. I have reduced them to the size of a nonstick omelet pan, about 8 inches in diameter, to incur less risk in the kitchen. Served at room temperature or slightly warm, they are a perfect contorno for the Braciolona, as they soak up the juices but don't become soggy while resting under the main event.

Boil the potatoes whole in plenty of water until tender, about 35 minutes; drain. While still warm, peel the potatoes and pass them through a food mill into a mixing bowl. Add the ricotta, provolone, eggs, and parsley and season with salt and plenty of black pepper.

With wet hands form eight 6-inch pizze about ½ inch thick. Place the bread crumbs on a plate. Press both sides of each pizza into the bread crumbs to coat.

Heat 1 tablespoon of oil in an 8-inch nonstick pan until smoking. One pizza at a time, cook the pizze until dark golden brown on both sides, about 4 minutes per side. Add more oil and adjust heat as needed to brown evenly. Place the cooked pizze on a tray lined with paper towels to drain until all are done.

To serve, place the pizze on a rack set on a cookie sheet. Crisp in a 450°F. oven for 6 to 8 minutes. Pile on a platter and serve hot with the Braciolona.

CIPOLLE RIPIENE

Stuffed Onions

8 large **red onions**

Kosher salt and freshly ground **black pepper**

¾ cup extra-virgin **olive oil**

¾ pound **ground chuck**

½ cup freshly grated **caciocavallo cheese**

¼ cup fresh **marjoram leaves**

½ cup **dry red wine**

1¼ cups fresh **bread crumbs**

Serves 8

Stuffed vegetables are great for a party because you can make them three days in advance and hold them in the coldest part of the refrigerator. If you want to make them vegetarian, or to lighten the meal, substitute 1 cup of freshly chopped herbs and 1 cup of fresh bread crumbs for the beef. (Photograph page 103.)

Preheat the oven to 425°F.

Carefully cut the onions exactly in half across the equator. Peel the onions and slice the smallest possible amount off the point end so the halves will stand upright. Stand the halves upright on a cookie sheet, season with salt and pepper, and drizzle with ¼ cup of the oil. Bake until just softened, about 15 minutes.

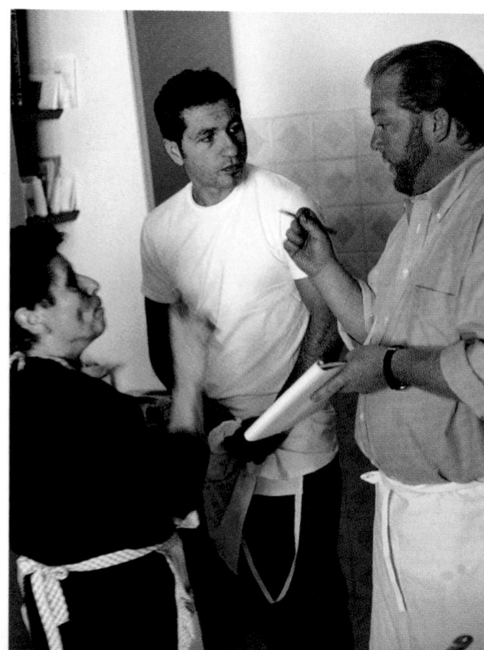

Dig out the center of each onion half with a spoon, leaving a ¼-inch-thick shell. Chop the inner layers and set aside.

In a 12- to 14-inch sauté pan, heat ¼ cup oil over medium heat until smoking. Add the ground chuck and cook, breaking up any chunks, until the fat has rendered and the meat has started to brown, 20 to 25 minutes. Drain the fat and add the chopped onions. Continue cooking over low heat until the onions are very soft, 15 to 20 minutes. Transfer the meat mixture to a bowl. Add the caciocavallo, marjoram, red wine, and ¾ cup of the bread crumbs, stir to mix well, and season with salt and pepper.

Carefully stuff each of the onion halves with the beef mixture, filling them just over the edge. Sprinkle with the remaining bread crumbs. Place the onions in a well-oiled glass baking dish, drizzle with the remaining oil, and bake until dark golden brown on top, 20 to 25 minutes. Serve hot. These also make a great light lunch served at room temperature with a simple salad.

SFORMATO DI CARDI

Cardoon Custard

A sformato is any vegetable-based custard in a ring or mold. Cardoons are nearly as easy to find in New York City as artichokes, but may take a search elsewhere in the country. They are seasonal and at Lupa and Babbo we usually start to serve them around the end of October. I find their flavor reminiscent of both artichokes and fennel, but different from each. If you cannot find them, substitute fennel or celery. (Photograph page 103.)

- 5 **cardoon stalks,** 1 to 1½ pounds
- ¼ cup extra-virgin **olive oil**
- 1 medium **red onion,** cut into ¼-inch dice
- 3 cups **Besciamella Sauce** (page 96)
- 5 **eggs** plus 2 **yolks**
- ½ cup **ricotta**
- ½ cup freshly grated **Parmigiano-Reggiano**
- Freshly grated **nutmeg**
- **Kosher salt** and freshly ground **black pepper**
- 2 tablespoons unsalted **butter**
- ¾ cup toasted fresh **bread crumbs**

Serves 8

Bring 6 quarts of water to a boil and add 2 tablespoons of salt. Peel the fibrous part of the cardoon stalks and cut each stalk on the bias into ¼-inch pieces. Drop the pieces into the boiling water and cook until tender, about 15 minutes. Drain and allow to cool.

Preheat the oven to 350°F.

In a 12- to 14-inch sauté pan, heat the oil over medium heat until smoking. Add the onion and cook until soft and light golden brown, 7 to 9 minutes. Add the cooked cardoon pieces and cook until very soft, about 10 more minutes. Remove from the heat and cool.

Transfer the cardoon mixture to a mixing bowl, add the Besciamella, eggs and yolks, ricotta, and ¼ cup Parmigiano, and season with nutmeg and salt and pepper. Butter 8 4-ounce ramekins and sprinkle with ½ cup of the toasted bread crumbs. Pour the cardoon mixture into the prepared ramekins and place in a roasting pan. Pour enough cool water into the roasting pan to come halfway up the sides of the ramekins and place in oven. Bake until the custards are just cooked through, and a toothpick stuck in the center exits clean, about 45 minutes. Allow to rest 10 minutes before edging the custards with a thin knife and turning them out onto a plate. Sprinkle with the remaining ¼ cup toasted bread crumbs and remaining grated cheese. Serve warm.

AFFOGATO AL CAFFE

Coffee Semifreddo "Drowned" in Coffee

SEMIFREDDO

2½ cups whole **milk**

3 ounces very strong **espresso**

6 **egg yolks**

1 cup **sugar**

1 tablespoon **vanilla extract**

2 cups **heavy cream**

8 cups strong decaffeinated **coffee,** cooled

¼ cup **unsweetened cocoa powder**

Serves 8

We have served this dessert at Pó for six years and it is consistently my favorite—a kind of adult milkshake. Be careful to use decaf for the bathing liquid, or your guests may be up yakking all night.

In a 3-quart saucepan bring the milk to a boil over medium-high heat. Remove from heat and add the espresso.

In a mixing bowl, beat the yolks until pale yellow. Gradually add the sugar and beat until light yellow ribbons form when the beaters are lifted. Stir in half of the hot milk, then stir in the remaining milk. Cook over low heat without boiling until the mixture coats the back of a spoon thickly and sets slightly, about 4 to 5 minutes. Stir in the vanilla and chill for ½ hour.

Whip 1½ cups of the cream to stiff peaks and fold into the custard mixture. Transfer to an ice cream machine and freeze according to manufacturer's instructions. (The semifreddo can be made up to 2 weeks in advance.)

Whip the remaining ½ cup cream to soft peaks. Place 1 scoop of semifreddo in each of eight tall glasses. Pour 1 cup of cooled coffee over each scoop, dollop with whipped cream, and dust with cocoa.

SANGUINACCIO

Cinnamon Chocolate Pudding with Pine Nuts

1 cup **unsweetened cocoa powder**

⅓ cup all-purpose **flour**

1½ cups **sugar**

4½ cups whole **milk**

12 ounces **semisweet chocolate,** coarsely grated

1 teaspoon **vanilla extract**

1 teaspoon ground **cinnamon**

5 tablespoons **pine nuts,** baked for 8 minutes in a 400° F. oven

Makes 10 6-ounce servings

Sticklers for authenticity would thicken this pudding with fresh pigs' blood; I thought that you'd prefer the recipe without it. Either way, it's a killer dessert.

Mix the cocoa powder, flour, and sugar in a mixing bowl. Slowly whisk in a bit of the milk to form a paste, then add the remaining milk to make a thin batter. Transfer to a large saucepan and, stirring constantly over medium heat, slowly bring to a boil. Remove from heat and add the grated chocolate, vanilla, and cinnamon and stir to mix well. When the chocolate is completely melted, fill 10 6-ounce ramekins four-fifths full, and allow to cool. Sprinkle each with the pine nuts and serve or chill until needed.

PIZZELLE

Thin Waffle Cookies

6 **eggs**

1 cup **sugar**

¾ cup vegetable **oil**

3 cups all-purpose **flour**

1 tablespoon **baking powder**

3 tablespoons **fennel seeds**

OPTIONAL

¼ cup **unsweetened cocoa powder** and 1 additional **egg,** OR

¼ cup **amaretto** and an additional ¼ cup **flour**

Makes 4 to 5 dozen

Grandma always sent lots of these and it wasn't until college that I discovered their true brilliance as part of the Nutella pizzelle sandwich!! These also make great cones for ice cream; simply wrap them around a conical dowel while still warm.

NOTE: You will need a pizzelle iron to make these cookies.

In a large bowl, combine the eggs, sugar, and oil and combine thoroughly. Add the flour, baking powder, fennel seeds, and the optional ingredients if desired, and mix well to form a homogeneous batter. Set aside at room temperature for 30 minutes.

Heat the pizzelle iron until very hot. Pour 2 tablespoons of batter onto the iron, close it, and return to heat. Cook until golden brown, about 2 minutes. Repeat until all the batter is used.

DIGESTIVI

After-Dinner Drinks

Having a little something to drink, probably of an alcoholic nature, is a very Italian way to end a meal. The most basic after-dinner drink (and the most common) is whatever is left in your glass from the meal—perhaps with a biscotti or two to dunk in the remnants. And certainly coffee in various guises is present at every Italian table. In fancier locales, however, *digestivi,* or digestifs, are offered. Meant to aid in the digestion of a massive lunch or dinner, these are often bitter or tonic-tasting. Many are herb-based and have an earthy flavor that is an acquired taste for some. In Amalfi, the *digestivo* of choice is limoncello. Although it's now available worldwide, limoncello was once the exclusive product of Capri, where it was invented. It is a relatively simple concoction, made from grain alcohol or vodka in which lemon peels have been steeped and to which a sugar syrup has been added. When served in a chilled glass, at the proper temperature—that is to say, almost freezing—limoncello is refreshing, almost slushy, like a grown-up version of the melting popsicles that dripped down your arm on a summer afternoon.

Grappas are another after-dinner offering and can be as rough or as soft as you like. I like to flavor grappa with fruits or spices and serve them in a series of small tastings, called a flight. Make some of your own for a completely unique ending to a special holiday meal.

Caffé

In Italy, *caffé* really means espresso, which is enjoyed by every member of the family at all times of the day. When it comes to serving, though, less is more. An espresso might be "stained" with foamed milk to make a *macchiato,* or fortified with more foamed milk to make a *cappuccino,* and even swollen with more milk to make a *caffé latte,* but that's generally as fancy as Italians get with their coffee: no caramel or toffee swirls, no boysenberry-flavored roasts, nothing in which powdered cocoas or whipped cream play a role. They will, however, ask for a "correction." *Caffé corretto* implies that the espresso has been "corrected" with a small shot of grappa or sambuca.

FLAVORED GRAPPAS

FLAVORINGS (CHOOSE 1):

Zest of 6 **oranges**

Zest of 8 **lemons**

6 **cinnamon sticks**

¼ cup **cardamom pods**

2 **quinces,** quartered and roasted with 4 tablespoons of sugar at 350° F. for 1 hour

2 **pears,** quartered and roasted with 4 tablespoons of sugar at 350° F for 20 minutes

¼ cup **star anise**

½ cup **dried cherries**

2 cups inexpensive grappa

Choose any one of the above options and place in a large jar with the grappa to steep for two weeks, stirring daily. At the end of the two weeks, strain out any fresh or roasted fruit bits (there is no need to strain out the spices) and store the flavored grappa in a decorative bottle.

NEW YEAR'S

The best part of New Year's Day is waking up and knowing that this is truly a national holiday. I look forward to making delicious food and enjoying it all day long, eating some of my favorite things without rush or intrusion, save the college bowl games. That said, I also reserve the right to doze during even the most exciting games, fading in and out till the fourth quarter, when all of the chips come down. This means that I need to plan menus that do not require a great deal of last-minute cooking.

Actually, this is less a menu than a full day of food and family activities. Each of these courses can be mapped out according to the needs of the day. I make the Eggs in Purgatory right before the first bowl game, around 9:30, and relax with friends who stayed over from New Year's Eve dinner. If you have a Balsamic Bloody Mary at this point, how could the day possibly go wrong? The Linguine with Walnut Sauce is a great light lunch. Making our own sausage is a New Year's Day

DAY

APERITIVO

BALSAMIC BLOODY MARY

ANTIPASTI

INSALATA DI MARE
Seafood Salad with Chickpeas and Olive Pesto

CALZONE DI RICOTTA E SCAROLA
Ricotta and Escarole Calzones

UOVA IN PURGATORIO
Eggs in Purgatory

PASTA

LINGUINE ALLE NOCI
Linguine with Walnut Sauce

PENNE ALLA GENOVESA
Pasta Served with Beef Cooked in an Onion Ragù

SECONDI E CONTORNI

SALSICCE FRESCHE CON PEPERONI
Fresh Homemade Sausage with Sweet Peppers

VERZO IMBOTITO
Cabbage Stuffed with Provolone

CARCIOFI RIPIENI
Stuffed Artichokes

BIGNE RUSTICHE
Cauliflower and Anchovy Fritters

DOLCI

BIANCOMANGIARE
Almond Clouds in Vanilla Almond Milk

CROSTATA DI MARMELLATA DI PRUGNE
Plum Preserve Tart

TORTA CAPRESE
Chocolate, Almond, and Walnut Tarts

REGALI: SNACKING ITALIAN STYLE
Cheese and Salami, Minestra Maritata

tradition in my family; around 1:00, I prepare the sausage and the peppers for later, and maybe have an afternoon snack of the stuffed artichokes and the cauliflower fritters with a glass of Fiano di Avellino. As the afternoon wanes I have a little salami, followed by the Penne alla Genovesa and maybe a little salad with some shaved Parmigiano and a glass or two of wine.

Before the big game at 8:00 I serve the main meal: the sausages, spaghetti with peppers, and the stuffed cabbage; by halftime I'm ready for the desserts and some Moscato d'Asti.

The beauty of planning the day like this is that no one is tied in one place too long. A day-long open house shouldn't exclude anyone from the festivities—least of all the host. It also means that you don't have to return to the same tired buffet as it ages hour after hour. New food and wine opportunities present themselves throughout the day. Plan to spend plenty of cooking and eating moments with the ones you love, in the kitchen, in front of the games, prepping the sausages and watching the peppers together, down in the cellar getting more wine, or bringing up more salami and cheese. It's the new year, Buon Anno Nuovo!

WINE RECOMMENDATIONS

Appetizers sing out for an elegant and plumy rose like Mastroberardino Irpinia Rosato Lacrimarosa, served slightly chilled. Other wines to consider for the rest of the day's festivities:

REDS

Terra di Lavoro, *1997 Fattoria Galardi*

Falerno del Massico 1997, *Villa Matilde*

Cecubo, *1996 Villa Matilde*

Aglianico di Taburno, *1995 Ocone*

WHITES

Fiano di Avellino Radici, *Mastroberardino 1998*

Fiano di Avellino Campo Re, *Terradora 1998*

Fiano di Avellino Struzziero 1998

Greco di Tufo Loggia della Sera Terredora 1998

Falerno del Massicio White Ville Matilde 1998

Falanghina Beneventano Sireum Mastroberardino 1998

Coda di Volpe Irpinia Marianna 1998

SWEET

Irpinia Privilegio, *Feudi di San Gregorio 1997*

Fiano di Avellino Pietracalda Vendemmia Tardiva Feudi di San Gregorio 1998

Greco di Tufo Cutizzi Vendemmia Tardiva Feudi di San Gregorio 1998

BALSAMIC BLOODY MARY

In a large pitcher, combine the vegetable cocktail, celery seed, pepper, citrus juices, 2 tablespoons of the horseradish, the Worcestershire sauce, and Tabasco and stir well to combine. Cover and refrigerate for 1 hour.

Fill 4 glasses with ice. Add 2 ounces of vodka to each and fill three-quarters full with the vegetable cocktail. Sprinkle with the remaining horseradish, place 1 celery stalk in each glass, and squeeze a lime wedge over each glass before dropping the wedge into the glass. Float a teaspoon of balsamic vinegar on the top of each drink and serve.

24 ounces **vegetable cocktail,** like V-8

1 teaspoon **celery seed**

1 tablespoon freshly ground **black pepper**

Juice of 1 **lime**

Juice of 1 **lemon**

3 tablespoons freshly grated **horseradish**

1 teaspoon **Worcestershire sauce**

Tabasco sauce to taste

8 ounces **vodka**

4 **celery stalks,** with leaves

1 **lime,** cut into wedges

4 teaspoons **balsamic vinegar**

Serves 4

INSALATA DI MARE

Seafood Salad with Chickpeas and Olive Pesto

Everyone makes seafood salad, and every version is unique. Here's how I like it. An Amalfitana would choose her ingredients from the fish market the morning of the meal. I've suggested seafood that should not be too difficult to obtain most times of the year. The octopus you will probably need to special-order, or substitute your favorite sea dweller—perhaps steamed lobster?

1½ cups **dry white wine**

2 pounds **mussels,** scrubbed and debearded

2 **lemon** slices

1 pound **calamari** tubes and tentacles, tubes cut into ¼-inch rings

½ pound medium **shrimp,** peeled

1 **wine cork**

1 pound baby **octopus,** 8 to 12 total

1 16-ounce can **chickpeas,** drained, rinsed, and drained again

1 medium **red onion,** halved and thinly sliced into half-moons

¾ cup extra-virgin **olive oil**

Scant ¼ cup **red wine vinegar**

2 tablespoons **green olive paste**

Generous tablespoon of freshly ground **black pepper**

2 **blood oranges** cut into segments

Serves 8

Place 1 cup of the wine in a 4-quart pot with a lid. Add the mussels, cover, and cook over high heat until they have steamed completely open, 5 to 6 minutes. Allow the mussels to cool, straining and reserving the steaming liquid separately.

In a 6-quart pot, bring 5 quarts of water to a boil with the lemon slices and the remaining ½ cup wine. Set up two bowls with 2 cups of ice and 2 cups of water in each. Plunge the cleaned calamari into the boiling liquid and cook until just opaque, 45 to 60 seconds, then remove from water with a skimmer or slotted spoon and immediately plunge into the ice water. Stir to stop the cooking quickly. Allow the calamari to cool in ice bath for 2 to 3 minutes, then drain carefully in a fine-mesh colander. Place in a 4- to 6-quart mixing bowl and set aside. Plunge the shrimp into the same boiling water and cook for 1 to 2 minutes, until completely orange. Remove to the second ice bath and cool as above. Drain the shrimp and add to the same bowl with the calamari; refrigerate.

Add a wine cork to the same boiling water, then add the octopus and return a boil. Lower the heat to just below the boil and simmer the octopus until tender, 45 to 50 minutes. Remove and allow to cool for 10 minutes, uncovered. Remove the beaks from the octopus using needle nose pliers, then carefully cut each octopus in half and add to the calamari and shrimp.

Carefully remove the mussels from their shells and add to the bowl. Add ¼ cup of the mussel-cooking liquid, the chickpeas, onion, olive oil, vinegar, green olive paste, and black pepper and gently stir shellfish to dress. Marinate for 20 minutes, then serve with the blood orange segments scattered on top. (This dish may be made up to 8 hours in advance, but don't add the vinegar more than 1 hour before serving.)

CALZONE DI RICOTTA E SCAROLA

Ricotta and Escarole Calzones

Traditionally, calzones in Campania contain only prosciutto and ricotta. In this very fancy holiday version, the currants and pine nuts are clear evidence of North African influence. Use a pizza stone to bake these savory pies for the best results in crustland. This is often served at room temperature but can also be eaten hot out of the oven.

DOUGH

¼ cup light **red wine** or **white wine**

¾ cup warm **water**

1½ ounces **yeast**

1 tablespoon **honey**

1 teaspoon **kosher salt**

1 tablespoon extra-virgin **olive oil**

3 cups all-purpose **flour**

FILLING

1 large head **escarole,** 1¼ to 1½ pounds

¼ cup extra-virgin **olive oil**

4 **garlic cloves,** thinly sliced

4 tablespoons tiniest **capers,** rinsed 3 times in water and drained

8 marinated **anchovy fillets,** finely chopped (see page 22)

1 cup **Gaeta olives,** pitted but left whole

¼ cup dried **currants**

¼ cup **pine nuts**

2 cups fresh **ricotta**

Kosher salt and freshly ground **black pepper**

2 **eggs,** well beaten

Makes 4 calzones; serves 8 as an antipasto

To make the dough: Combine the wine, water, and yeast in a large bowl and stir until dissolved. Add the honey, salt, and the olive oil and mix thoroughly. Add 1 cup of the flour and mix with a wooden spoon to make a loose batter. Add 2 more cups of the flour and stir with the spoon for 2 to 3 minutes to incorporate as much flour as possible.

Bring the dough together by hand and turn out onto a floured board or marble surface. Knead for 6 to 8 minutes, until you have made a smooth, firm dough. Place the dough in a lightly oiled bowl and cover with a towel. Set aside to rise in the warmest part of the kitchen for 45 minutes.

For the filling: Bring 3 quarts water to a boil. Separate the escarole leaves and rinse thoroughly. Drop leaves into the boiling water and cook until tender, 8 to 9 minutes. Drain and allow to cool. Stack the leaves and cut into 1-inch ribbons.

In a 12- to 14-inch sauté pan, heat the ¼ cup of oil over high heat until smoking. Add the garlic and cook 2 to 3 minutes, until light golden brown. Add the capers, anchovies, olives, currants, and pine nuts and cook 2 to 3 minutes, until the garlic is dark golden brown but not burnt. Add the escarole and stir until well mixed and cook until very soft, 10 to 14 minutes. Remove from the heat and allow to cool. Gently stir in the ricotta and season the mixture with salt and pepper.

Cut the risen dough into 4 equal pieces and knead each portion into a round. Cover again and let rest 15 minutes.

Preheat the oven to 450°F. Place a clean pizza stone in oven to preheat.

Dust a clean work surface lightly with flour. With your fingers and palms, flatten one of the dough rounds into a 10-inch oval about ⅛ to ¼ inch thick. Place one quarter of the escarole mixture just above the center of each oval. Fold the dough to form a half-moon and then press the edges to seal. Fold the edge up with your fingertips and pinch closed to form a ridge all the way around. Repeat with the remaining dough and filling. Brush with the beaten egg. Place the calzones directly on the pizza stone and bake 15 to 18 minutes, until golden brown. Serve hot or cool to room temperature.

UOVA IN PURGATORIO

Eggs in Purgatory

¼ cup extra-virgin **olive oil**

1 medium **red onion,** thinly sliced

½ cup **Gaeta olives,** pitted and left whole

1 28-ounce can peeled **plum tomatoes,** drained and cut into into ½-inch strips

Kosher salt

10 **eggs**

¼ cup **basil** cut into thin ribbons

¼ cup freshly grated **caciotta cheese**

Serves 6 to 10

I like this simple egg dish for New Year's Day because it makes the hungover guests feel like they didn't miss breakfast when they show up at 3:00 in the afternoon. Once cooked, the eggs can sit for a while at room temperature.

In a 12- to 14-inch nonstick sauté pan, heat the oil over medium heat until just smoking. Add the onion and cook until softened and light brown, 7 to 9 minutes. Add the olives and tomatoes, season lightly with salt, and cook slowly until the tomatoes start to break down, about 15 minutes.

Carefully crack the eggs into the pan, keeping them whole and separated from each other. Cover the pan with a lid or foil and cook until the egg whites have set but the yolks are still runny, 3 to 4 minutes. Sprinkle with basil and grated cheese and serve from the pan.

LINGUINE ALLE NOCI

Linguine with Walnut Sauce

¼ cup extra-virgin **olive oil**

3 **garlic cloves,** thinly sliced

½ cup toasted hard **bread crumbs**

1 cup roughly chopped **walnuts**

1 tablespoon hot red **pepper flakes**

1 pound **linguine**

½ cup roughly chopped **Italian parsley**

½ cup freshly grated **caciocavallo cheese** or pecorino romano

Serves 4 to 8

The texture of mixed nuts and bread crumbs makes this an ethereal pasta. When the noodles are cooked and then dressed just right, they taste great even at room temperature.

Bring 6 quarts of water to a boil and add 2 tablespoons kosher salt

In a 14- to 16-inch fry pan, heat the oil over medium heat till smoking. Add the garlic and cook until light golden brown, 2 to 3 minutes. Add half of the bread crumbs, the walnuts, and pepper flakes and cook until lightly toasted, 3 to 4 minutes. Remove from the heat and set aside.

Drop the pasta into the boiling water and cook according to the package instructions until 1 minute short of al dente. Just before draining the pasta, add ¼ cup of the pasta cooking water to the pan with the walnut mixture.

Drain the pasta in a colander and pour the pasta into the pan with the walnut mixture. Place the pan over medium heat and continue cooking the pasta with the walnut mixture until the pasta is lightly dressed with the condiment, about 1 minute. Add the parsley and grated cheese, stir through, pour into a heated bowl, sprinkle with the remaining bread crumbs, and serve immediately.

PENNE ALLA GENOVESA

Pasta Served with Beef Cooked in an Onion Ragù

Here's another great two-for-the-price-of-one dish that yields a savory sauce for dressing pasta, plus a substantial beef roast to slice and serve as a main dish. The beef is braised in a liquid that very nearly resembles French onion soup.

- 1½ ounces **pancetta**
- 1 ounce **salami**
- 1 ounce **proscuitto**
- ¼ cup extra-virgin **olive oil**
- 2 pounds boneless top round of **beef,** tied at regular intervals with butcher's twine
- 5 large **Spanish onions,** thinly sliced
- 3 medium **carrots,** coarsely chopped
- 2 **celery stalks,** coarsely chopped
- 1 16-ounce can peeled **tomatoes,** crushed, and their juices
- **Kosher salt** and freshly ground **black pepper**
- 1¼ cups **dry white wine**
- 1 pound **ziti** or **rigatoni**

Makes 4 to 8 pasta servings, 8 meat servings for later

Mince the pancetta, salami, and prosciutto together to form a paste. In a large, heavy-bottomed pot, heat the olive oil and add the minced meats. Cook over medium heat to soften but not color. Add the beef and brown well on all sides so that a deep brown crust is formed. Remove the beef and set aside.

To the same pan, add the onions, carrots, and celery and cook 1 to 2 minutes, to soften but not brown. Add the tomatoes, ½ teaspoon salt, and wine and bring to a simmer, scraping the bottom of the pot with a wooden spoon to loosen the browned bits. Return the beef to the pot, cover tightly, and cook over low heat for 2½ hours or until the meat is fork-tender. Remove the meat from the pan and allow to rest 15 minutes before serving.

Bring 6 quarts of water to a boil and add 2 tablespoons salt. Cook the pasta according to package directions, until 1 minute short of al dente. Drain the pasta and add it to the pan with the meat sauce. Toss over high heat 1 minute to coat the pasta. Serve the pasta first, then the meat.

SALSICCE FRESCHE CON PEPERONI

Fresh Homemade Sausage with Sweet Peppers

FOR THE SAUSAGE

4 pounds fresh boneless **pork shoulder,** coarsely ground

2 pounds **pancetta,** coarsely ground

2 tablespoons freshly ground **black pepper**

4 tablespoons **kosher salt**

2 tablespoons **fennel seed**

1 tablespoon hot red **pepper flakes**

2 tablespoons **hot paprika**

½ cup **dry white wine**

8 feet salt-packed **sheep's casings,** about ½ pound

FOR THE PEPPERS

6 tablespoons extra-virgin **olive oil**

1 medium **red onion,** cut into thin slices

5 red and 5 yellow **bell peppers,** seeded, cored, and cut into ½-inch strips

1 tablespoon hot red **pepper flakes**

2 tablespoons dried **oregano**

1 can **tomato paste**

1 cup **dry red wine**

1 small bunch **chives**

Makes 24 links; serves 8

In my family, sausage making is a New Year's Day tradition. My father continues on that road with his own *salumeria* called Armandino's Salumi, located just off Seattle's Pioneer Square. He makes traditional sausages and salami as well as original creations like lamb prosciutto and pig cheek soppressata. Have your butcher grind the meats on the largest possible setting; otherwise the results will be more like hotdogs than sausage.

NOTE: The casings must be soaked in cool water overnight to remove the salt before using.

Make the sausage: In a mixing bowl, stir together the pork shoulder and pancetta with your hands until well mixed. Add pepper, salt, fennel seed, pepper flakes, paprika, and wine and mix until well blended, again with your hands. You must move quickly here or your body temperature could change the texture of the fat. Set up the sausage stuffer and place the casing over the funnel feeder. (If you do not have a sausage stuffer, you need to buy one, but, for today, you can just form the sausage into ¼-pound logs by hand and be more careful handling them.) Stuff the sausage into the casings, twisting every 3½ to 4 inches (about 4 ounces each) and form 22 to 25 sausages.

Make the peppers: In a 12- to 14-inch sauté pan, heat the oil over medium heat till smoking. Add the onion, bell peppers, pepper flakes, and oregano and cook until softened, 8 to 10 minutes. Add the tomato paste and cook until paste turns darker, 15 to 18 minutes. Add the wine and simmer 10 minutes. Remove from the heat and allow to cool.

To finish the dish, place a 14- to 16-inch skillet over medium heat. Prick the sausages all over with a needle and place them in the pan. Cook over medium heat until dark golden brown on the bottom, 7 to 9 minutes, moving them frequently. Turn the sausages and add the pepper mixture. Bring to a boil, lower the heat, and simmer for 15 to 20 minutes, adding water, ¼ cup at a time as needed to keep the consistency like that of a sauce. Remove the sausages to a warm plate and keep warm.

Arrange the peppers on a platter, top with the sausages and the chives.

MADE IN ITALY

VERZO IMBOTITO

Cabbage Stuffed with Provolone

My "gourmet" friends usually snicker when they see stuffed cabbage in my kitchen, but their laughs are quickly stifled when they taste this succulent vegetarian version. The only trick is buying the right capers and provolone—both must come from Italy. These packets may also be served at room temperature for a light lunch.

1 large **green cabbage,** 3 to 4 pounds

6 tablespoons extra-virgin **olive oil**

2 medium **red onions,** cut into ½-inch dice

2 tablespoons salt-packed **capers,** rinsed and drained

1 cup whole **Gaeta olives,** pitted

Kosher salt and freshly ground **black pepper**

2 cups fresh **bread crumbs**

1½ pounds young **provolone cheese,** cut into ½-inch cubes

3 **garlic cloves,** thinly sliced

2 cups **Basic Tomato Sauce** (page 97)

½ cup freshy grated **pecorino cheese**

1 bunch fresh **basil,** cut into thin ribbons

Makes 12 rolls

Preheat the oven to 375°F. Bring 8 quarts of water to a boil in a large pot. Fill a large bowl with cool water.

Remove the tough outer leaves of the cabbage and set aside for cole slaw. Carefully cut out the cabbage core with a sharp knife, then drop the whole cabbage into the boiling water. Cook until tender and flexible, but not completely "cooked," 6 or 7 minutes, then remove and refresh in the cool water. Carefully remove the whole leaves and set aside about a dozen of the best and largest. Chop the remaining cabbage into ¼-inch pieces and set aside.

In a 12- to 14-inch sauté pan, heat the oil over medium heat until just smoking. Add the onions and the chopped cabbage and cook until very soft, 12 to 15 minutes, stirring occasionally. Add the capers and the olives and cook another 5 minutes. Season with salt and pepper to taste and allow to cool.

When the onion mixture is cool, add bread crumbs, provolone, and garlic and delicately fold together. Check for seasoning.

Place a scant ½ cup of the filling mixture in the center of each whole cabbage leaf. Fold like a burrito and secure with a toothpick.

Pour the tomato sauce into a 9- by 12-inch baking dish and arrange the cabbage packets on top. Add ½ cup water. Cover the dish tightly with foil and bake for 30 minutes. Remove the foil, sprinkle the rolls with the grated pecorino, and bake another 20 minutes. Sprinkle with the basil and serve from the baking dish.

CARCIOFI RIPIENI

Stuffed Artichokes

- 8 jumbo **artichokes**
- Juice of 2 **lemons**
- 3 cups **dry white wine**
- 5 **garlic cloves,** thinly sliced
- 1½ bunches fresh **thyme**
- ¼ cup extra-virgin **olive oil**
- 1 large baking **potato,** cut into ¼-inch dice
- 2 pounds fresh **favas beans,** shelled and peeled
- 2 **scallions,** thinly sliced
- ½ cup fresh **bread crumbs**
- ¼ pound **salami,** cut into ⅛-inch dice
- ¼ cup coarsely chopped **Italian parsley**
- **Kosher salt** and freshly ground **black pepper**

Makes 16

Stuffed vegetables are a bit time-consuming to prepare, but the investment pays off when you see how easy it is to put something so impressive on the table. I recommend making these a day or two ahead and hiding them in the back of the fridge, as they're impossible to resist. (Photograph page 130.)

Remove the outer layer of leaves from the artichokes and cut the artichokes in half. Use a small knife to remove the spiny choke.

In a large saucepan, combine 4 quarts of water, the lemon juice, 2 cups of the wine, the garlic, and ½ bunch thyme and bring to a boil. Add the artichokes and blanch for 20 minutes, until tender. Drain, cool; and set aside.

Preheat the oven to 375°F.

In a 12- to 14-inch sauté pan, heat the oil until almost smoking. Add the potato and cook, stirring gently, until soft and light golden brown, about 10 minutes. Add the fava beans and scallions and cook for 4 to 5 minutes. Remove from heat, add the bread crumbs, salami, and parsley, and mix well to combine.

Season the cavity of each artichoke with salt and pepper and stuff with the potato mixture. Place the artichokes in a shallow baking dish, add the remaining 1 cup of wine and 1 bunch thyme, and cook for 30 minutes. Serve immediately, or serve at room temperature as an antipasto.

BIGNE RUSTICHE

Cauliflower and Anchovy Fritters

This batter is called pâte choux in France and looks a lot like beignets when it's cooked in New Orleans, but be not afraid! It's really simple and makes a dramatic presentation out of simple cauliflower. (Photograph page 130.)

1 cup **water**

1 teaspoon **kosher salt**

½ cup (1 stick) unsalted **butter**

1 cup all-purpose **flour**

4 **eggs**

2 small heads **cauliflower,** about 1½ pounds, cut into 1-inch florets

8 salt-packed **anchovies,** soaked, rinsed, and filleted (see page 25)

2 quarts **olive oil,** for deep frying

Makes 25 to 30 fritters

Combine the water, salt, and butter in a 2-quart saucepan and bring to a boil. Have a whisk and a wooden spoon ready. Remove the pan from the heat and add the flour all at once, whisking it in. Return to the heat and start stirring with the wooden spoon. Cook, stirring constantly, until the dough starts to pull from the sides of the pan and form a ball, about 3 minutes. Remove from the heat and stir until tepid, 6 to 8 minutes. Add the eggs, one at a time, incorporating each one completely before adding the next. Pour into a mixing bowl, cover with plastic wrap, and set aside at room temperature.

Bring 4 quarts of water to a boil and fill a bowl with 3 cups of ice and 4 cups of water. Plunge the cauliflower into the boiling water and cook until tender (not al dente) 8 to 10 minutes. Remove and refresh in the ice bath. Drain the cauliflower pieces well, dry on a kitchen towel, and place in a mixing bowl. Chop the anchovy fillets very fine and add to the cauliflower; stir to distribute. Add the cauliflower mixture to the batter and stir gently to mix well.

Heat the oil to 375°F. in a 6- to 8-quart pot. Line a baking sheet with several layers of paper towels and preheat the oven to 200°F. Using two tablespoons, form fritters by grabbing a floret of cauliflower with a generous amount of the batter that adheres. Drop the fritter into the hot oil. Cook six or seven at a time until golden brown, flipping them with a slotted spoon. Remove to the prepared baking sheet and keep warm in the oven while you fry the remaining fritters. Serve hot.

BIANCOMANGIARE

Almond Clouds in Vanilla Almond Milk

These little flavor powerhouses are destined to replace panna cotta as the next hip dessert in post-tiramisù Italian restaurants. The almond-infused milk is as rich and intense as it is light and sexy, and does spectacular double duty as the base of this dessert and its sauce.

1½ envelopes unflavored **gelatin**

½ pound blanched **almonds**

6½ cups whole **milk**

Zest of 2 **lemons**

2 cups **sugar**

2 tablespoons **almond oil**

1 cup **heavy cream,** very cold

1 tablespoon **vanilla extract**

1 **egg** plus 4 **yolks**

Seeds from 1 **pomegranate**

Makes 10 6-ounce custards

Place the gelatin in 2 cups of cold water and set aside. Place the almonds in a food processor and grind to a powder. Combine the milk and lemon zest in a nonreactive saucepan. Add the ground almonds and bring to a boil over medium-high heat. Remove from the heat, cover, and let stand 20 minutes.

Line a sieve with cheesecloth and strain the milk mixture, pressing with the back of a spoon to remove all of the liquid; discard the solids.

Set aside 1½ cups of the flavored milk for the sauce and place the remaining milk, 1½ cups of the sugar, and the soaked gelatin in a saucepan. Bring just to a boil, stirring constantly, remove from the heat immediately, and allow to cool to room temperature.

Grease ten 6-ounce ramekins with the almond oil and set aside. Whip the cream to soft peaks and fold the cooled almond milk and vanilla into the whipped cream. Spoon the mixture into the greased molds up to 90 percent full and refrigerate for at least 4 hours.

Meanwhile, beat together the egg and the egg yolks. Add to the remaining reserved flavored milk and add the remaining ½ cup sugar. Place over medium heat and, stirring constantly, heat to a high simmer, 175°F. Remove from heat, pour through a strainer into a small bowl, and refrigerate 1 hour.

To serve, dip the bottoms of the molds in a bowl of hot water, being careful not to allow any water to go over the edge into the mold, and carefully invert onto large plates. Sometimes you need to run a sharp knife around the perimeter of the custard to loosen it from the mold.

Whisk the sauce to loosen it and pour over the custards. Garnish with pomegranate seeds and serve.

CROSTATA DI MARMELLATA DI PRUGNE

Plum Preserve Tart

MARMELLATA

4 pounds **plums,** peeled, pitted, and cut into 1/4-inch half-moon slices (red prune plums preferred, but locally grown is best)

2 cups **sugar**

Juice and grated zest of 1 **lemon**

PASTRY

3 cups all-purpose **flour**

3/4 cup **sugar**

1 1/2 sticks (3/4 cup) unsalted **butter,** cut into 1/4-inch cubes

Scant 1/2 cup chilled **white wine**

1/2 cup **orange marmalade**

Makes 2 9-inch tarts

Italian culture holds home preserving in high esteem. Making marmalades or jams throughout the spring and summer seasons allows the home cook the luxury of serving tarts with summer flavor all year long. I definitely recommend using a top-quality store-bought jam over buying out-of-season fruit, as a substitute for the homemade marmellata.

Make the marmellata: In a nonreactive pan, combine the plums, sugar, and juice and zest of lemon and bring to a boil over medium heat. Lower the heat and simmer for 45 minutes. Pour into sterilized jars, and refrigerate for up to 3 weeks. Or can fruit using your favorite recipe.

Make the pastry: Mound the flour and sugar on a wooden board, and form into a well. Place the butter pieces in the well and mix using your fingers (quickly so as not to melt the butter) until the butter and flour mixture resembles bread crumbs. Add the chilled wine and mix to bring the dough together. When it just holds a shape, wrap the dough in plastic and refrigerate for 20 minutes.

Preheat the oven to 375°F.

Roll out the dough using a rolling pin to form two 10-inch circles about 1/2 inch thick, repairing holes or tears with pieces from an outer edge. Place the crusts in two 9-inch tart pans. Allow the dough to rest for 20 minutes in the refrigerator. Cover the pastry with sheets of waxed paper and fill with dried beans. Bake in the oven till the pastry is medium golden brown, about 20 to 25 minutes, then remove from the oven and allow to cool.

Remove the waxed paper and beans and fill each shell with 2 cups of the marmellata. Heat the orange marmalade with 4 tablespoons of water to boiling and brush over a thin coating with a pastry brush. These tarts are ready to be eaten but can last up to 2 days in the pantry.

TORTA CAPRESE

Chocolate, Almond, and Walnut Tarts

These tarts are in the window of every pastry shop in Naples the week before Christmas, and I'm quite certain that they all use this very recipe. They do, however, decorate them with different patterns of confectioners' sugar or cocoa. Regardless of the paint job, this is an impressive finish and one that rivals any "flourless" chocolate cake recipe.

1 cup (2 sticks) unsalted **butter,** softened

1 cup **granulated sugar**

10 **eggs**

¼ pound blanched, sliced **almonds**

¼ pound **walnut halves**

4 ounces **semisweet chocolate,** grated

Confectioners' sugar, for dusting

Serves 10

Preheat the oven to 400°F. Butter and flour a 10-inch tart pan with straight sides.

Place the butter and granulated sugar in a mixer and beat on high speed until light yellow and fluffy, 7 to 9 minutes. Lower the mixer to medium and beat in the eggs, until a light ribbon is formed. Remove the bowl from the mixer and stir in the almonds and walnuts with a spatula. Add the grated chocolate, mix well, and pour into the prepared pan.

Bake until set, about 40 minutes. Remove to a wire rack and cool in the pan. Turn out the tart onto a serving dish and sprinkle with confectioners' sugar.

Alternatively, arrange five 4-inch tart pans on a baking sheet. Fill with the batter and bake for 20 to 25 minutes. This tart can be made the day before and held in an airtight container.

SNACKING ITALIAN STYLE

Cheese and Salami

Snacking is a ubiquitous holiday pastime in my home and indeed in any Italian home. Snack foods tend to be a bit more ribsticking than mere chips or handful of peanuts; a small plate of pasta at room temperature, a stuffed calzone, or a bowl of hearty meat-and-vegetable soup that has simmered on the stove throughout the holiday preparations would fit the bill perfectly. The most obvious choice, and for me one of the tastiest, is a few slices of salami and a chunk or two of cheese.

When it comes to the etymology of their cheeses, Italians tend to recognize the process rather than the result. *Pasta filata*, a term used to categorize certain soft, fresh cheeses, means "spun paste," a nod to the way these cheeses are manipulated by hand to achieve their characteristic consistency. *Mozzarella*, one such cheese, comes from the Italian verb *mozzare*, to tear, which could also be an inadvertent reference to the way American mass-producers have destroyed the image and integrity of this cheese with their plastic bricks of tasteless, rubbery shreds.

Ricotta, which means "re-cooked," is traditionally made from the whey, practically a by-product of cheese making, which is then heated again with a coagulant to form the creamy stuff of which southern Italian dreams are made.

Salami, on the other hand, is an open field. Soppressata may contain game or organ meats in some regions and be simply a fatty pork sausage in others. The term *salumi* refers to all salted and preserved meats, primarily made from pork, and Italy's tradition of artisanal salami-making is considered a national treasure, the individual recipes passed down through the generations. To be served one of these special meats is the ultimate sign of hospitality.

MINESTRA MARITATA

Big-Time Meat and Vegetable Soup

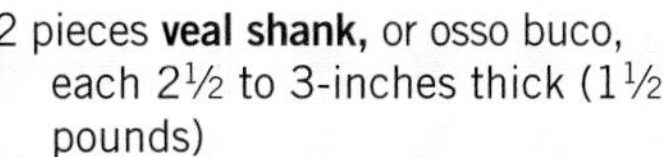

- 2 pieces **veal shank,** or osso buco, each 2½ to 3-inches thick (1½ pounds)
- 1 2½ to 3-pound **chicken**
- 2 large **pork ribs** (1½ pounds)
- ½ pound spicy **salami,** in one piece
- ½ pound **soppressata,** in one piece
- 4 fresh **Italian sausages**
- ½ pound **pancetta,** in one piece
- 1 **carrot,** peeled and halved
- 2 **celery stalks,** halved
- 1 large **onion,** halved
- 1 bunch each of **thyme, rosemary,** and **parsley**
- 3-inch piece **Parmigiano Reggiano** rind
- ½ pound hard **caciocavallo cheese**
- 1 hot **dried pepper,** or 1 tablespoon hot red **pepper flakes**
- 1 head **escarole,** cut into ½-inch thin ribbons
- 1 bunch **cima di rape** or **broccoli rabe,** cut into ½-inch pieces
- 1 bunch **curly endive,** cut into ¼-inch thin ribbons
- **Kosher salt** and freshly ground **black pepper**
- Grated **pecorino cheese,** for garnish
- ¼ cup **Olio Piccante** (page 57)

Serves 8 to 10

In a giant soup pot combine the veal shanks, chicken, pork ribs, salami, soppressata, sausages, pancetta, carrot, celery, onion, herbs, cheese rind, caciocavallo, and hot pepper. Cover with 3 gallons of water, place over high heat, and bring to a boil. Lower the heat and simmer for 2 hours, augmenting the water occasionally to keep the meats submerged. Gently remove all of the meats and the cheese and cheese rind and allow to cool. Cover and refrigerate. Strain the broth, discarding the vegetables and herbs, and refrigerate overnight.

The next day, skim off the solidified fat that has risen to the top of the broth. Remove the veal, chicken, and pork from the bones, and cut all the meat and sausages into ¾-inch pieces. Cut the Parmigiano rind and the caciocavallo into ¼-inch cubes. Bring the broth to a boil in a soup pot and add the escarole, rabe, and endive. When it boils, add all of the meat and cheese pieces.

Return to a boil, then lower the heat and simmer for 1 hour. Season, if necessary, with salt and pepper. Allow to rest 1 hour, covered, then serve with grated pecorino and a drizzle of Olio Piccante.

The following are some of my favorite sources for the top-quality food products that are essential to preparing a flawless holiday meal.

ARTHUR AVENUE CATERERS

Cured meats, specialty items, cheeses.

2344 Arthur Avenue, Bronx, NY 10458
(718) 295-5033

BALDUCCI'S

Cheeses, cured meats, fish, produce, olive oils, vinegars.

Mail-order catalogue: (800) 225-3822

Retail store:

424 Sixth Avenue (at West 9th Street)
New York, NY 10011
(212) 673-2600
www.balducci.com

THE CHEESE STORE OF BEVERLY HILLS

Cheeses, wine, truffles and truffle products, oils, vinegars.

Mail-order catalogue: (800) 547-1515

419 North Beverly Drive, Beverly Hills, CA 90210
(310) 278-2855

www.cheesestorebh.com

D'ARTAGNAN

Fresh game and poultry.

280 Wilson Avenue, Newark, NJ 07105
(800) 327-8246

www.dartagnan.com

DEAN AND DELUCA

Cured meats, cheeses, olive oil, vinegar, blood orange juice, specialty produce.

Mail-order catalogue: (800) 221-7714

Retail stores:

560 Broadway, New York, NY 10012
(212) 226-6800

607 South St. Helena Highway, St. Helena, CA 94574
(707) 967-9980

www.dean-deluca.com

DIPALO

Italian cheeses (including 85 types of pecorino), cured meats, olives, oil, vinegar, pasta.

206 Grand Street, New York, NY 10002
(212) 226-1033

FAICCO

Cured meats, dry pasta, oils, vinegar.

Retail store:

260 Bleecker Street, New York, NY 10014
(212) 243-1974

FORMAGGIO KITCHEN

Cheeses, olive oils, vinegars, pasta, specialty foods.

Mail-order catalogue: (888) 212-3224

Retail store:

244 Huron Avenue, Cambridge, MA 02138
(617) 354-4750

ISCHIA

Italian cheeses, cured meats, olives, oils, vinegars, pasta, spices.

Mail-order catalogue: (718) 446-0134

5-12 37th Avenue, Woodside, NY 11377

MURRAY'S CHEESE SHOP

Extensive cheese selection, olives, oils, vinegar, pasta, imported specialty items.

Mail-order catalogue: (888) 692-4339

Retail store:

257 Bleecker Street, New York, NY 10014
(212) 243-3289

www.murrayscheese.com

ARMANDINO'S SALUMI

Extensive selection of house-made and cured salami.

Retail store:

309 Third Avenue South, Seattle, WA 98121
(206) 621-8772

URBANI TRUFFLES AND CAVIAR

Fresh and dried mushrooms, truffles, truffle oil, caviar.

Mail-order catalogue: (800) 281-2330

29-24 40th Avenue
Long Island City, NY 11104

www.urbani.com

ZABAR'S

Cheeses, cured meats, fish, produce, specialty items.

Mail-order catalogue: (800) 697-6301

Retail store:

2245 Broadway (at West 80th Street)
New York, NY 10024
(212) 787-2000

www.zabars.com

ZINGERMAN'S

Cheeses, specialty items, olive oils, vinegars, produce.

422 Detroit Street, Ann Arbor, MI 48104
(734) 769-1625

INDEX

CONVERSION CHART

American cooks use standard containers, the 8-ounce cup and a tablespoon that takes exactly 16 level fillings to fill that cup level. Measuring by cup makes it very difficult to give weight equivalents, as a cup of densely packed butter will weigh considerably more than a cup of flour. The easiest way therefore to deal with cup measurements in recipes is to take the amount by volume rather than by weight. Thus the equation reads:

1 cup = 240 ml = 8 fl. oz. ½ cup = 120 ml = 4 fl. oz.

It is possible to buy a set of American cup measures in major stores around the world.

In the States, butter is often measured in sticks. One stick is the equivalent of 8 tablespoons. One tablespoon of butter is therefore the equivalent to ½ ounce/15 grams.

LIQUID MEASURES

Fluid Ounces	U.S.	Imperial	Milliliters
	1 teaspoon	1 teaspoon	5
¼	2 teaspoons	1 dessertspoon	10
½	1 tablespoon	1 tablespoon	14
1	2 tablespoons	2 tablespoons	28
2	¼ cup	4 tablespoons	56
4	½ cup		110
5		¼ pint or 1 gill	140
6	¾ cup		170
8	1 cup		225
9			250, ¼ liter
10	1¼ cups	½ pint	280
12	1½ cups		340
15		¾ pint	420
16	2 cups		450
18	2¼ cups		500, ½ liter
20	2½ cups	1 pint	560
24	3 cups		675
25		1¼ pints	700
27	3½ cups		750
30	3¾ cups	1½ pints	840
32	4 cups or 1 quart		900
35		1¾ pints	980
36	4½ cups		1000, 1 liter
40	5 cups	2 pints or 1 quart	1120

SOLID MEASURES

U.S. and Imperial Measures		Metric Measures	
Ounces	Pounds	Grams	Kilos
1		28	
2		56	
3½		100	
4	¼	112	
5		140	
6		168	
8	½	225	
9		250	¼
12	¾	340	
16	1	450	
18		500	½
20	1¼	560	
24	1½	675	
27		750	¾
28	1¾	780	
32	2	900	
36	2¼	1000	1
40	2½	1100	
48	3	1350	
54		1500	1½

OVEN TEMPERATURE EQUIVALENTS

Fahrenheit	Celsius	Gas Mark	Description
225	110	¼	Cool
250	130	½	
275	140	1	Very Slow
300	150	2	
325	170	3	Slow
350	180	4	Moderate
375	190	5	
400	200	6	Moderately Hot
425	220	7	Fairly Hot
450	230	8	Hot
475	240	9	Very Hot
500	250	10	Extremely Hot

Any broiling recipes can be used with the grill of the oven, but beware of high-temperature grills.

EQUIVALENTS FOR INGREDIENTS

all-purpose flour–plain flour
coarse salt–kitchen salt
cornstarch–cornflour
eggplant–aubergine
half and half–12% fat milk
heavy cream–double cream
light cream–single cream
lima beans–broad beans
scallion–spring onion
unbleached flour–strong, white flour
zest–rind
zucchini–courgettes or marrow